Return to the Lord

Return to the Lord

A Lenten Journey of Daily Reflections

Mark G. Boyer

ALBA · HOUSE   NEW · YORK

SOCIETY OF ST. PAUL, 2187 VICTORY BLVD., STATEN ISLAND, NY 10314

Library of Congress Cataloging-in-Publication Data

Boyer, Mark G.
    Return to the Lord : a Lenten journey of daily reflections / by
Mark G. Boyer.
        p.   cm.
    ISBN 0-8189-0605-7 : $8.95
    1. Lent — Prayer-books and devotions — English.   2. Lent-
-Meditations.   3. Catholic Church — Prayer-books and devotions-
-English.   I. Title.
    BX2170.L4B695   1991
    242'.34 — dc20   90-24013
                                                                                    CIP

Designed, printed and bound in the United States of
America by the Fathers and Brothers of the
Society of St. Paul, 2187 Victory Boulevard,
Staten Island, New York 10314, as part of their
communications apostolate.

Printing Information:

Current Printing - first digit   1   2   3   4   5   6   7   8   9   10   11   12

Year of Current Printing - first year shown
 1991   1992   1993   1994   1995   1996   1997   1998

DEDICATED TO

my double uncle and double aunt,
Thomas A. and Thelma A. Boyer,
my godparents.

TABLE OF CONTENTS

Third Sunday Of Lent

Fourth Sunday Of Lent

Fifth Sunday Of Lent

Holy Week

The Easter Triduum

Appendix

INTRODUCTION

The title of this book is *Return to the Lord: A Lenten Journey of Daily Reflections*. The word "return" implies that one has been away. This is true for all of us, no matter what degree of holiness we may have achieved. Because we are human, we sometimes wander away from God. Lent is the time to return.

"Lord" is another name for God. At one time it was a title given only to the most powerful. Once people began to realize that it was God who saved them, they began to recognize God's supreme power, and they named God "Lord." To the Lord we return during Lent.

Lent is a forty-day journey. As the "Commentary on the General Norms for the Liturgical Year and the Calendar" states, "The biblical significance was the greatest factor in determining this number of days in which Christians would prepare themselves for the feast of the Lord's Passover."[1]

The "Commentary" explains, "Our Lord fasted forty days; God's people spent forty years in the desert; Moses remained on Mount Sinai forty days; for forty days Goliath threatened Israel until David stood forth and slew him; Elijah, nourished only with a cake baked on hot stones and a jar of water, took forty days to travel to Mount Horeb; and finally, Jonah spent forty days preaching to the Ninevites."[2]

This book is meant to be a guide for the Christian pilgrim as he or she makes this year's forty-day Lenten journey.

The Constitution on the Sacred Liturgy, issued by the bishops during Vatican Council II on December 4, 1963, made the foci of Lent clear — "the recalling of baptism or the preparation for it, and penance."[3] According to this document, "It is by means of them that the Church prepares the faithful for the celebration of Easter, while they hear God's word more frequently and devote more time to prayer."[4]

These two foci guide the choice of Scripture texts for the Lenten Season. "The readings for the Sunday Masses . . . present . . . the prophets' call to repentance, and . . . provide . . . every three years . . . a synthesis of the total mystery of salvation. . . . During Lent the entire Church, together with those who will be baptized, recalls the mystery of Christian initiation."[5]

The weekday selections of Scripture "treat various themes of the Lenten catechesis that are suited to the spiritual significance of this season."[6]

By recalling baptism, by "pointing out the social consequences of sin," and by impressing "on the minds of the faithful the distinctive character of penance as a detestation of sin because it is an offense against God,'"[7] unique Lenten Scriptures guide us through the forty-day Lenten journey to the fifty-day Easter feast. Thus, "the Lenten liturgy disposes both catechumens and the faithful to celebrate the paschal mystery."[8]

This book can be used by individuals for daily, private reflection and prayer and by homilists for daily, public liturgical preaching and prayer. A six-part exercise is offered for every day for the Lenten Season and for the Easter Triduum.

1. A few short verses of Scripture are taken from the first reading provided in the *Lectionary for Mass* of each day.

2. All of the Scriptures of the Mass for each day are noted. Thus, those wishing to examine the connection between the readings can do so with ease.

3. A reflection follows the list of readings. The reflection is an attempt to expand an idea or an image found in the verses from the Scriptures; it can be used as the starter for a homily, or it can easily be considered as a homilette in itself.

4. The reflection is followed by a question for personal meditation. The question functions as a guide for further development of the idea or image chosen in the reflection. Also, it challenges us to delve deeply into ourselves and to see how the Scripture interprets our life.

The homilist can use the question to develop a homily or pose it to the congregation for its reflection. After the question a suitable time of silence should be allowed for meditation.

5. A prayer summarizes the original theme of the Scripture, which was expanded in the reflection and which served as the basis for meditation. The prayer can conclude the daily exercise for the individual, or it can be used as a fitting conclusion to the General Intercessions and the Liturgy of the Word during the celebration of the Eucharist.

6. The sixth part of the daily exercise consists of an activity. This section provides questions, whose written answers are meant to be kept in a personal journal. These questions further expand the meditation and push the reader to seriously consider his or her past experiences which are associated with the Scripture, reflection, meditation, and prayer. Through this written record one can see where he or she has traveled on the forty-day Lenten pilgrimage.

One feast and two solemnities interrupt the Lenten Season. The Feast of the Chair of Peter, Apostle, occurs on February 22. If Ash Wednesday falls after this date, as it frequently does, then this feast is outside of Lent. However, during some years, the feast interrupts Lent. In this case, a six-part exercise can be found in the Appendix.

The Solemnity of Joseph, Husband of Mary, on March 19, and the Solemnity of the Annunciation of the Lord on March 25 always interrupt the Lenten Season unless they occur during Holy Week, in which case they are transferred to the first free liturgical day. A six-part exercise for both of these solemnities can also be found in the Appendix.

Because of the mobility of these three days, it is best to check a Catholic calendar, which names the feasts and the solemnities. In this way, the reader will know if and when to celebrate these three days during Lent.

The date for Easter Sunday is determined by the moon. Easter is always the first Sunday after the first full moon following the Spring equinox. Once Easter Sunday is determined, then six Sundays are counted backward, and the Wednesday before the first of the six Sundays preceding Easter is Ash Wednesday. Because of the mobility of Ash Wednesday and Easter Sunday, the following table is provided.

Year	Sunday Cycle	Ash Wednesday	Easter Sunday
1991	B	February 13	March 31
1992	C	March 4	April 19
1993	A	February 24	April 11
1994	B	February 16	April 3
1995	C	March 1	April 16
1996	A	February 21	April 7
1997	B	February 12	March 30
1998	C	February 25	April 12
1999	A	February 17	April 4
2000	B	March 8	April 23

The color of Lent is the deep violet of preparation and repentance. It is meant to foster quiet and solemn introspection. Purple sends one to fasting, prayer, and almsgiving. It indicates that the joy of the "Alleluia" is removed for forty days so that people can prepare with mind and heart for the celebration of the Easter Triduum and the Easter Season. Lent is an invitation, which is sent to everyone. It reads: "Return to the Lord."

Notes

1 *Norms Governing Liturgical Calendars,* "Commentary on the General Norms for the Liturgical Year and the Calendar," Liturgy Documentary Series 6, Office of Publishing and Promotion Services, United States Catholic Conference, 1312 Massachusetts Avenue, N.W., Washington, DC 20005-4105, p. 65.

2 Ibid.

3 "The Constitution on the Sacred Liturgy," *Vatican Council II: The Conciliar and Post-Conciliar Documents,* Study Edition, Austin Flannery, General Editor, Costello Publishing Co., Inc., PO Box 9, Northport, NY 11768, paragraph 109.

4 Ibid.

5 Liturgy Documentary Series 6, p. 67.

6 *Lectionary for Mass: Introduction,* Liturgy Documentary Series 1, Office of Publishing Services, United States Catholic Conference, 1312 Massachusetts Ave., N.W., Washington DC 20005-4105, paragraph 98.

7 "The Constitution on the Sacred Liturgy," paragraph 109.

8 "General Norms for the Liturgical Year and the Calendar," Liturgy Documentary Series 6, paragraph 27.

Return to the Lord

TRUMPET

Scripture: Blow the trumpet in Zion!
            proclaim a fast,
            call an assembly;
        Gather the people,
            notify the congregation;
        Assemble the elders,
            gather the children
            and the infants at the breast . . .
                                                    (Joel 2:15-16)

Mass: Joel 2:12-18; 2 Corinthians 5:20-6:2;
        Matthew 6:1-6, 16-18

Reflection: When one hears the sound of a trumpet, he or she takes notice. A trumpet heralds the fact that something important is about to take place. People are drawn toward the sound of a trumpet, if not out of curiosity then out of a desire to be with everyone else, rushing toward the trumpet blast.

Ash Wednesday is the trumpet of the Church. This day heralds a six-week period of fasting, praying, and almsgiving. Such deeds, however, are not done alone or for the sake of individuals, but as and for the assembly, the community, the body of Christ. The Ash Wednesday trumpet calls the whole community together in order that the entire congregation may find its heart reoriented toward the Lord. Fasting, prayer, and almsgiving are the means to this reorientation.

The Ash Wednesday trumpet call reminds everyone of the need to reassemble. It is a blast that awakens us from our post-Christmas, wintertime sleep. The blown trumpet is a reminder of the need that all of us have for a time of reform. Thus, Ash Wednesday begins in miniature one aspect of what our whole life in the community should constantly consist — fasting, prayer, and almsgiving.

Meditation: To what type of lifestyle is the Ash Wednesday trumpet calling you?

Prayer: Merciful God, you are gracious, slow to anger, rich in kindness, relenting in punishment, and you always have pity on your people when they accept your constantly offered gift of grace. Now is the time for us to turn back to you. Today is the day of salvation. Move our hearts to repentance through fasting, prayer, and almsgiving. Leave behind your blessing upon us, Father, Son, and Holy Spirit, one God living and reigning forever and ever. Amen.

Activity: Draw up for yourself a plan for fasting during Lent. On your calendar indicate which days you will fast and from which foods you will fast. Why are these foods your choices?

CHOICES

Scripture: "Here, then, I have today set before you life and prosperity, death and doom . . . , the blessing and the curse. Choose life, then, that you and your descendants may live, by loving the Lord, your God, heeding his voice, and holding fast to him."
(Deuteronomy 30:15, 19-20)

Mass: Deuteronomy 30:15-20; Luke 9:22-25

Reflection: The life of every man, woman, and child is filled with choices which must be made yearly, monthly, weekly, daily and, sometimes, hourly. Yearly, one must decide whether or not to renew the life insurance policy. Monthly, a decision must be reached whether or not to continue to subscribe to the same trash pick-up service. On a weekly basis one must decide where the best grocery prices are offered. Daily, a person has to make a decision concerning work. Sometimes, especially in a hospital emergency, a decision concerning an operation must be made quickly, occasionally within the hour.

Hidden somewhere within each choice that must be made is another choice between life and death, or prosperity and doom, or blessing and curse. In other words, we always have the option to choose that which will provide the most life or that which will provide the most death. What is the guide in all this decision-making? Love of God is the guide. By loving God we open ourselves to God's guidance; we heed God's voice and hold fast to him. Those who love God are guided by him to choose that which will insure a long life.

Meditation: What choice do you need to make at this moment in your life? Which option represents life? Which option represents death?

Prayer: God of life, prosperity and blessing, you set before us multiple choices that we might choose to love you, to keep your ways, commandments, statutes, and decrees. Guide our hearts that we might not be led astray and perish. Fill us with your word that we might have a long life and inherit the promises which you made to Abraham and Sarah, Isaac and Rebekah, Jacob and Leah and Rachel. We ask this through Christ our Lord. Amen.

Activity: Make a list of all the choices that you make during this day. Categorize them according to choices for life and choices for death. Do you have more choices for life or more choices for death?

FASTING

Scripture: Is this the manner of fasting I wish,
of keeping a day of penance:
That a man bow his head like a reed,
and lie in sackcloth and ashes?
Do you call this a fast,
a day acceptable to the Lord?
This, rather, is the fasting that I wish:
releasing those bound unjustly,
untying the thongs of the yoke;
Setting free the oppressed,
breaking every yoke;
Sharing your bread with the hungry,
sheltering the oppressed and the homeless;
Clothing the naked when you see them,
and not turning your back on your own.
(Isaiah 58:5-7)

Mass: Isaiah 58:1-9; Matthew 9:14-15

Reflection: When we hear the word "fast," we most likely and immediately think of eating. For most of us, fasting implies consuming less food for a day or more. Today, many people fast as part of diet and health center programs. In other words, they fast in order to lose weight.

While this is a laudatory form of fasting, it is not what the prophet Isaiah had in mind. Isaiah calls on us to fast from gossip and derogatory remarks. He tells us that we are to break the yoke of long-held grudges and past hatreds; this will require us to fast from words. We must stop looking in at the storefront windows asking ourselves, "What do I need?" and start looking out of our own windows at the hungry, the homeless, and the naked and begin to provide them with what they need. By fasting from buying another consumer item, we may be able to feed or shelter or clothe the oppressed.

Authentic fasting does not involve just the self. Authentic fasting is a way of clearing away obstacles that prevent us from seeing our neighbor in need. In other words, fasting reduces us all to the same common, human denominator!

Meditation: Do you fast for yourself? Or, do you fast for others?

Prayer: Lord, you promise that when we cry for help that you will answer and say, "Here I am!" We have sinned against you and our brothers and sisters. Guide our fasting according to your vision; then, enable us to set free the oppressed, to share bread with the hungry, to shelter the homeless, and to clothe the naked. Make our light break forth like the dawn and heal our sinful wounds. Permit us to see the glory you share with your Son, our Lord Jesus Christ, and your Holy Spirit, one God, forever and ever. Amen.

Activity: Identify one way in which you can fast and share your bread with the hungry. Identify one way in which you can fast and shelter the homeless. Identify one way in which you can fast and clothe the naked.

BREAD

Scripture: If you bestow your bread on the hungry
and satisfy the afflicted;
Then light shall rise for you in the darkness,
and the gloom shall become for you like midday;
Then the LORD will guide you always
and give you plenty even on the parched land.
He will renew your strength,
and you shall be like a watered garden,
like a spring whose water never fails.

(Isaiah 58:10-11)

Mass: Isaiah 58:9-14; Luke 5:27-32

Reflection: The word "bread" is used in multiple ways. It can refer to the tight-textured homemade bread which has been carefully kneaded by a loved one. It can refer to the light, air-filled loaf, which can be found wrapped in cellophane on the shelves of the grocery store. It can imply whole wheat, dark, bran, or bleached varieties. Bread can take the form of bagels, muffins, rolls, etc. All of these represent the type of bread that all of us eat.

Bread can also be used in reference to one's livelihood. To earn one's daily bread is to bring home a paycheck every week or month. Sometimes, one's earnings — the money itself — is called bread. Money enables us to purchase the bread — food, clothing, shelter — we need.

Bread is meant to be broken and shared with others. A freshly baked loaf of bread invites people to come and tear off a piece and taste it. Rolls are usually placed in a basket from which all can share. One's earnings are brought home in order to share them with family and friends.

However, there is still a wider circle of family and friends who are in need of bread. These are the hungry and the afflicted. As long as there are poor — those without bread — on the earth, every one of us has an obligation to break off a small portion of our loaf of bread and offer it to those who have none.

Meditation: Where can you offer some time, talent, or treasure in order to share your bread with others?

Prayer: God of bread, when your people hungered for food in the wilderness, you sent them manna — bread from heaven — so that they had plenty, even in the parched land. Open our eyes that we might see those who have no bread. Make our light of generosity shine in the darkness of hunger. Renew our strength that we might share your gifts and become like you, a watered garden, a spring whose generosity never fails. We ask this through Christ our Lord. Amen.

Activity: Make a list of five blessings — bread — that you have. After each blessing list one way in which you can share this bread with others.

Cycle A

GARDEN

Scripture: Out of the ground the LORD GOD made various trees grow that were delightful to look at and good for food, with the tree of life in the middle of the garden and the tree of the knowledge of good and bad.

(Genesis 2:9)

Mass: Genesis 2:7-9; 3:1-7; Romans 5:12-19; Matthew 4:1-11

Reflection: All of us have a "garden," a favorite place where we can relax, put up our feet and bask in silence. This garden might be a physical yard which is surrounded by blossoming plants, or it might be an easy chair which is placed next to a window through which the quiet of the world can be viewed. No matter what form the garden takes, in it there are a variety of things that are delightful. These things serve as nourishment for our spirit.

When we go to our garden, we may take along a book or a newspaper to read. The book provides entertainment if a novel, or information if a textbook, or insight if spiritual reading, or meditation if the Bible. A newspaper keeps us up-to-date on world events. This in itself is a type of nourishment.

Sometimes we may take nothing to the garden but our thoughts. In this case, garden time is thinking time. Thoughts are delightful to look at and good for food. A decision that needs to be made can be thought through in the garden. A solution to a problem can be reached with some time spent in the garden.

Sometimes we may invite another person into our garden. Husbands and wives go to the garden together in order to foster their love relationship. Friends take each other to a garden to explore the uniqueness of each other. Children find their gardens good places to bring playmates.

The garden is a place of mystery. It is where the knowledge of good and bad is attained. Reading, thinking, and loving are revolutionary acts. All provide knowledge, which must be judged as good or bad. In the midst of such garden activity, we must be careful not to play the role of God; to do so is to risk losing the innocence of the garden.

Meditation: Where is your garden? When were you last there? What did you do while there? Did you make decisions between what is good and bad, right for you or wrong?

Prayer: Lord God, once you planted a garden in Eden and placed there the man and woman you had formed from the dust of the earth. However they turned from your face and sinned; they wanted to be like you, able to decide for themselves the difference between right and wrong. Through the death and resurrection of Jesus you have restored our lost innocence. Make us faithful stewards of your many gifts and fill us with a wisdom that comes from your Holy Spirit, who lives and reigns with you and your Son, our Lord Jesus Christ, one God, forever and ever. Amen.

Activity: Make a list of one book you need to read during this Lent, one decision you need to reach, and one friendship you need to foster in your garden. When are you going to do each of these?

Cycle B

RAINBOW

Scripture: God said to Noah and to his sons with him: "... This
is the sign that I am giving for all ages to come, of
the covenant between me and you and every living
creature with you: I set my bow in the clouds to
serve as a sign of the covenant between me and the
earth."
(Genesis 9:8, 12-13)

Mass: Genesis 9:8-15; 1 Peter 3:18-22; Mark 1:12-15

Reflection: It is not usual to see a rainbow in the sky. Rainbows
are not daily phenomena. It takes a special day with the rain
clouds in the right relationship to the sun for the bow to be
created. A truly magnificent bow displays the brilliant colors of
violet, blue, red, orange and yellow. A person can only stand in
awe before such a display of the spectrum.

It is no wonder, then, why primitive people chose the
rainbow as a sign of God's covenant with them. The light
reminded them of God. The bow, arched between heaven and
earth, reminded them of God's throne above and their own place
below. The bow served to unite heaven and earth.

The covenant was God's doing. God offered a promise of
life to his people. The bow was to be used as a reminder to God

to remember his promise to protect all of the life of the earth —
every living creature: birds and fish and wild and tame animals.

Even though a rainbow is not seen that often, God never
forgets the promise of life that was once made. Neither can we.
A deep appreciation for all life is necessary, if every living
creature is to continue to survive. Therefore, it is necessary to
conserve life — the lives of human beings, the lives of forests,
mountains, rivers, animals, and birds. Every time a rainbow is
lifted up in the sky all people should be reminded of the
covenant of life between themselves, God, and every living
creature and thing on the earth.

Meditation: In which ways do you adhere to the covenant of
life between God, every living creature and thing, and yourself?

Prayer: God of life, once you set your bow in the clouds to
serve as a sign of the covenant of life between yourself and the
earth. Give us a greater respect for life and the earth and
everything that exists on it. Help us to see the beauty of everything that has come from your hand. When we view your
rainbow in the sky, remind us of our duty to be faithful stewards
of all that you have made. We ask this through our Lord Jesus
Christ, your Son, who lives and reigns with you and the Holy
Spirit, one God forever and ever. Amen.

Activity: Make a list of three ways in which you can foster the
covenant of life between God and the earth. How can you
become a brighter rainbow?

Cycle C

EGYPT

Scripture: "The LORD, the God of our fathers . . . brought us
out of Egypt with his strong hand and outstretched
arm, with terrifying power, with signs and wonders;
and bringing us into this country, he gave us this
land flowing with milk and honey."

(Deuteronomy 26:7-9)

Mass: Deuteronomy 26:4-10; Romans 10:8-13; Luke 4:1-13

Reflection: Every person has known an Egypt, a land of slavery
and oppression. For one individual Egypt might have been a job
that he or she just hated. For another person Egypt might have
consisted of a possessive relationship. Being poor, homeless, an
alcoholic or a drug addict might have been Egypt for others. God
did not create people to live in such an Egypt.

No! God made us in his own image so that we could share
in the milk and honey of freedom. The first step to this new type
of life is a recognition and an ability to name the Egypt in which
one is afflicted or oppressed.

If it is a job that enslaves us, then perhaps a new job needs
to be found even though it is not easy to leave behind seniority,
health insurance plans and the comfortable feeling of knowing
the ropes.

If a relationship is the oppressor, then the two parties involved must sit down and work it out. It will not be easy to lay out authentic feelings and to honestly listen to and confront the other.

Likewise, if it is some addictive behavior — alcoholism, drug abuse, over-eating, sexual abuse — then we must be willing to say to ourselves that we have a problem and need help. It's not comfortable looking into the mirror and seeing our shortcomings and vulnerabilities, but it's necessary if a new life is to be embraced.

In the very process of recognizing the slavery, affliction, or oppression, we also get the first glimpse of the help that God offers. God waits for us at times to declare that a change is needed. Then he comes to deliver us from our Egypt. With God's strong hand, he grasps the hand of the downtrodden and leads them through the distress of job hunting. With his outstretched arm, God offers some security to the person who is trying to resolve a relationship which has gone sour. Those who are addicted find themselves witnessing signs of recovery and wonders of peace and reconciliation.

The end result of these changes is nothing other than a new life, a grand entry into the land flowing with milk and honey. The milk of freedom and the sweet honey of success await those who are willing to follow God as he leads them out of Egypt.

Meditation: In what Egypt do you currently find yourself? How can you escape?

Prayer: Lord, God of those who went before us, when our ancestors were held captive in Egypt, when they were afflicted and oppressed, they cried out to you and you delivered them from maltreatment. Hear our cries today. Deliver us from our slavery. With your strong hand and outstretched arm, with terrifying power, with signs and wonders, lead us into a new life, into a land flowing with milk and honey. We ask this through our Lord Jesus Christ, your Son, who lives and reigns with you and the Holy Spirit, one God forever and ever. Amen.

Activity: Make a list of three Egypts from which you have been delivered. Identify how God was at work leading your from captivity to freedom. Identify the new life that you now enjoy in the land flowing with milk and honey.

HOLINESS

Scripture: The LORD said to Moses, "Speak to the whole
Israelite community and tell them: Be holy, for I, the
LORD, your God, am holy. You shall love your
neighbor as yourself."   (Leviticus 19:1-2, 18)

Mass: Leviticus 19:1-2, 11-18; Matthew 25:31-46

Reflection: Holiness can be understood as the degree of our
relationship with God. The God of the Hebrews, of the Israelites, of the Jews, and of Christians wants us to enter into a
relationship with him. God wants us to get involved with him.
The degree of our involvement is holiness.

We are to get involved with God to the same degree that
God gets involved with us. From the creation of the first couple
to the present day, God has been actively at work among his
people. God called Abraham to leave his homeland and journey
to a new land. He called Moses to lead his people out of the land
of slavery into one of freedom. The pagan king, Cyrus, was
inspired by God to permit the Israelites to return from Babylon
to Jerusalem; Cyrus even helped in the rebuilding of the holy
city. In the human flesh of Jesus of Nazareth, God became even
more involved with his people.

God asks us as his people today to get involved with him.
One way of demonstrating this is by becoming holy. And we
become holy through the love of our neighbor. When we love

our neighbor, we do not steal, speak falsely, rob, defraud, curse, act dishonestly, or slander another. To do any of these things violates the law of love and robs us of the holiness to which we've been called.

Holiness, is not just a personal relationship with God — although it is this, too, of course. Holiness involves a communal relationship with God and with others. God speaks his commandments to the community and asks that the community respond in relationship and in holiness to each other. Thus, holiness is measured by the degree of our participation in the community first, then by our personal relationship with God.

Meditation: At what degree is your holiness?

Prayer: All-holy God, you never cease to offer yourself in love to your people. When they fall, you raise them up. When they fail, you forgive them. When they take the wrong path, you guide them back to the highway of your grace. Remove all evil from our midst and help us to keep your commandments. Enable us to love our neighbor as we love ourselves. We ask this through our Lord Jesus Christ, your Son, who lives and reigns with you and the Holy Spirit, one God, forever and ever. Amen.

Activity: Make a list of your actions which demonstrate your love of neighbor. Make a list of your actions which demonstrate a love of God. Make a list of your actions which demonstrate a love of yourself. Where do these lists intersect? How do these actions measure your holiness and that of your community?

POTENTIAL

Scripture: For just as from the heavens
                     the rain and snow come down
                 And do not return there
                     till they have watered the earth,
                     making it fertile and fruitful,
                 Giving seed to him who sows
                     and bread to him who eats,
                 So shall my word be
                     that goes forth from my mouth;
                 It shall not return to me void,
                     but shall do my will,
                     achieving the end for which I sent it.
                                                    (Isaiah 55:10-11)

Mass: Isaiah 55:10-11; Matthew 6:7-15

Reflection: A teacher will often speak of a student as having potential to be a great scientist or mathematician. A manager looks over his or her employees to see if any one of them has any potential to be promoted to a managerial position. The editor of a newspaper might tell a reporter that he or she has the potential to be a writer of fiction.

Potential is that which can develop. An acorn has the potential for becoming an oak tree. A tulip bulb has the potential for blossoming into a beautiful flower. There exists the potential for all people to hear God's word and to do it.

Yes, even God's word has potential; it can develop in individuals so that it becomes incarnate. In fact, God promises that the word from his mouth will achieve its potential, its foreordained end. It will develop into what God wants — a people who are eager and enthusiastic to do God's will.

The hidden potential in God's word is like the potential of the rain and snow, which water the earth and bring forth life. Those persons who hear God's word have the potential for fertile, fruitful, eternal life. Where there is no potential, there is only a void — emptiness — and there is no life.

Meditation: In which recent way has the word of God achieved its potential in your life?

Prayer: God of rain and snow, you send your gift of water to the earth so that the seed might grow and your people might have food to eat. You send the gift of your word to the earth so that your people might hear it and do your will. Open our ears to hear that which comes forth from your mouth. In the midst of so many other words, do not let yours become void, but bring the potential for doing your will to completion in us. We ask this through our Lord Jesus Christ, your Son, who lives and reigns with you and the Holy Spirit, one God, forever and ever. Amen.

Activity: Make a list of three ways in which God's word has reached its potential in you. What happened? How was the void in you turned into a fertile and fruitful life?

REPENTANCE

Scripture: Jonah began his journey through the city, and had gone but a single day's walk announcing, "Forty days more and Nineveh shall be destroyed," when the people of Nineveh believed God; they proclaimed a fast and all of them, great and small, put on sackcloth.   (Jonah 3:4-5)

Mass: Jonah 3:1-10; Luke 11:29-32

Reflection: What does it take to convince people of the need to repent, of the need to turn around, of the need to make changes in their lives? For some people a personal crisis leads to repentance. The crisis might consist of losing a job, the breaking up of a relationship, or the death of a loved one. During times of personal crisis many people discover themselves being changed. Someone offers a prospect for a new job. A friend appears seemingly from nowhere to offer comfort. Death is turned into hope for the fullness of eternal life.

For other people the hearing or reading of the word of God, the Bible, motivates repentance. It might be an old biblical story that has been heard a hundred times, but for some reason it is heard differently the hundred and first time around; the result is a change in one's life. While reading the holy book an individual might discover a truth whose depths lead him or her to alter his or her life.

Repentance can also be sparked by those who preach. Jonah is the envy of every evangelist. The city of Nineveh was so huge that it took three days to walk through it. This meant that Jonah would have to preach three full days in order to preach a few words to every citizen. However, after only one day of preaching the whole city repented. As signs of their repentance, the people proclaimed a fast and put on sackcloth.

Whoever or whatever it is that leads to repentance, the motivator behind it is God. God calls all of us to continual repentance, to continual change, to ongoing conversion. The presence of another person, the reading of the word of God, the preaching of the Scriptures, when they have the power of God behind them, lead us to that repentance.

Meditation: What recent event in your life has caused you to repent?

Prayer: God of Jonah, you filled your prophet with words from your own mouth and sent him to a foreign land in order to indicate your love for all men and women and your desire that everyone repent. After but one day of preaching, you gave success to your prophet's words, and the whole city of Nineveh proclaimed a fast and put on sackcloth. Open our ears to hear your word and turn our hearts to repentance that we might be transformed into the image of Jesus, your Son, who lives and reigns with you and the Holy Spirit, one God, forever and ever. Amen.

Activity: Make a list of three people who have caused great changes to take place in your life. What was the change which each person engendered? What kind of repenting did you do?

FALSE GODS

Scripture: Queen Esther, seized with mortal anguish . . . , had recourse to the LORD. "My LORD, our King, you alone are God. Save us by your power, and help me, who am alone and have no one but you, O LORD."

(Esther C:12, 14, 25)

Mass: Esther C:12, 14-16; 23-25; Matthew 7:7-12

Reflection: Not unlike ancient times, the world of today is filled with many gods, each competing with the other for recognition and worship. In the past, people bowed down to idols of stone and wood and brass. Today, the objects have changed, but the bowing down remains the same.

For some people television has become a god. It occupies the attention of the room within which it is placed. Most of the furniture is oriented toward the TV. Sometimes it is placed in its own shrine-like cabinet, so that its tabernacle-like doors can be solemnly opened to reveal its screen. Meals are eaten before it; conversations are held around it; some even fall prostrate on the floor before it.

Money is god for some people. Money is treated with the greatest of respect. Once it is received in the solemn form of a check, it is immediately deposited in its own shrine — the bank. Automatic tellers offer the possibility of removing it for viewing or spending anytime one desires. When it is carried in a purse or hip pocket, it is usually placed in a wallet or beneath a specially crafted money clip. Those who believe that money represents the gods of life and death spend lots of time managing it, investing it, enabling it to fill the vacuums of their life.

Another person can become a god. When a fellow human being becomes an idol, an example of someone to imitate, one held up to the general public for special adulation, he or she assumes divine status. Others flock to see this person on the baseball field, in concert or, if already deceased, tomb-side. Wherever the encounter takes place, sacred words are spilled, incantations are sung, and gifts — such as flowers, food, or money — are offered.

With so many other gods around, it is easy for Christians to forget that there is but one God who is invisible but, nevertheless, the real God. This God provides a world which is charged with his presence. He bestows gifts upon his people that are more lavish than money can buy. This God assumed human form and demonstrated how much more important trust and faith are than anything else. By recognizing their total dependence upon God, people touch the depths of their humanity and at the same time reach the heights of the divinity in whose image they are created.

Meditation: What false god do you find that you worship?

Prayer: Lord, our King, you alone are God. You never forget your people. In times of distress, manifest yourself to us and give us your gift of courage. Place on our lips the words you wish us to proclaim so that others may turn to you and recognize your love and care for all of your creation. Save us by your power, for alone we can do nothing. We ask this through our Lord Jesus Christ, your Son, who lives and reigns with you and the Holy Spirit, one God, forever and ever. Amen.

Activity: Make a list of the other gods that you find present in the world today. After each one indicate how you may unknowingly find yourself paying homage to it.

CONVERSION

Scripture: If the wicked man turns away from all the sins he committed, if he keeps all my statutes and does what is right and just, he shall surely live, he shall not die. And if the virtuous man turns from the path of virtue to do evil, the same kind of abominable things that the wicked man does, can he do this and still live?

(Ezekiel 18:21, 24)

Mass: Ezekiel 18:21-28; Matthew 5:20-26

Reflection: Conversion, a word used frequently in churches, can contain a number of meanings. Conversion can refer to an experience of faith which leads a person to adopt a particular religious expression. It can imply that a radical change has taken place in a person's life. The word might simply refer to some alteration in one's day-to-day activities.

Conversion can also mean reform, turning around, walking in a new direction. Throughout both Testaments of the Bible, God is interested in the reform of the lives of his people.

First, God is interested in those persons who are labeled "wicked." God is willing to forget totally all of a person's sins and crimes, if that individual adopts a new way of living — that is, is converted — and follows God's way of virtue.

Second, God is also interested in those who are labeled "virtuous," especially when they abandon God's ways in order to do evil. God is not willing to remember the virtue, though, in the face of broken faith. However, such a sinner can always return to his or her former life of good deeds and God is willing to forgive him or her.

God is interested in each of us and offers all of us the opportunity to reform our lives. Sometimes, instead of getting to work on the process of conversion, we begin to argue with God and accuse God of being unfair. In other words, we begin to set up standards for reform which are stricter than God's own. Conversion is a personal responsibility, although it is assisted and nurtured by a community of faith. However, each of us must accept the call to reform and stand ready to defend our own actions. The accusation that God's ways are unfair simply will not do when God asks to see the results of reform and conversion in our life.

Meditation: How do you need to reform your life?

Prayer: Lord God, you derive no pleasure from the death of the wicked, but you rejoice when the wicked turn from evil and you give them life. You take no pleasure when the virtuous turn away from following your ways, but rather you call them back to yourself. Remove our wickedness and give us the grace to reform our lives. Help us to know your will and to put it into practice. We ask this through our Lord Jesus Christ, your Son, who lives and reigns with you and the Holy Spirit, one God, forever and ever. Amen.

Activity: Make a list of three areas — either small, medium, or large — in your life that need change. After each provide the steps that you would have to take to accomplish this reform. Choose one and get busy working on it today.

COVENANT

Scripture: "Today you are making this agreement with the LORD: he is to be your God and you are to walk in his ways and observe his statutes, commandments and decrees, and to hearken to his voice. . . . You are to be a people peculiarly his own, as he promised you."

(Deuteronomy 26:17-18)

Mass: Deuteronomy 26:16-19; Matthew 5:43-48

Reflection: In the ancient world, a covenant was an agreement entered into between two people, one of whom was more powerful than another. Usually, the more powerful of the two initiated the covenant. This person had something to gain from the agreement, such as soldiers for an army, hands for the grain fields, servants for the household. The less powerful person welcomed such a covenant, because the benefits of food, clothing and shelter were assured by the one who was more powerful.

Through Moses, God entered into a covenant with the people he led out of Egyptian slavery to spiritual formation in the desert. Obviously God was the more powerful; the people, the community of Israel, the less powerful. The agreement, however, was simple. Israel would be a people who kept God's commandments, statutes, and decrees, a people peculiarly his own. In other words, Israel would belong to God and worship

God alone. The community of escaped and freed slaves would listen to God's voice.

What did God get out of the agreement? God promised the people that he would make them known among the other nations of the earth, and that they would be a people sacred to God. Israel would be held up in renown and glory by God. In other words, God would have a community to which the Lord alone belonged and in which he alone was worshiped.

The covenant made with Israel has been extended to every person on the earth. Every human being has been offered the invitation to be one who is peculiarly God's own. Jesus, God's Son, extended the covenant with his own blood on the cross. His followers, after his resurrection, announced to both Jews and Gentiles that what God had accomplished in Jesus was for the benefit of the entire human community. Such a move on the part of God, the more powerful partner in the agreement, was done solely out of his great love for people and his great mercy.

Today, God still desires that all people enter into the covenant with him. God still seeks a community willing to hear his word, keep his commands, and observe his statutes and decrees. God wants to make all people a people peculiarly his own.

Meditation: Today, how can you hear God's word, keep his commands, or observe his statutes and decrees?

Prayer: Lord, once you entered into a covenant with your chosen people. You asked them to listen to your voice, to keep your commands, and to observe your statutes and decrees; they would be a people peculiarly your own. Through Jesus, your Son, you have extended this covenant to every human being on the face of the earth. Grant us the grace to accept your gifts and to live as a people who always walk in your ways. May we await the day when you will raise us high in praise and renown and glory above all the earth. We ask this through our Lord Jesus Christ, who lives and reigns with you and the Holy Spirit, one God, forever and ever. Amen.

Activity: Make a list of the ways that you intend to keep the terms of God's covenant with you today.

Cycle A

SENT FORTH

Scripture: The LORD said to Abram: "Go forth from the land of your kinsfolk and from your father's house to a land that I will show you." (Genesis 12:1)

Mass: Genesis 12:1-4; 2 Timothy 1:8-10; Matthew 17:1-9

Reflection: People are always being sent forth. A UPS delivery person is sent forth with a truck full of packages. A taxi is sent forth to pick up and deliver precious human cargo. A missionary is sent forth to a foreign country to preach the gospel. The list of those who are sent forth is endless. Sending forth is a daily occurrence.

The model for being sent forth is Abram. As the author of the book of Genesis portrays him, Abram went forth from his own country to a new land, as the Lord directed him. He trusted that God would fulfill his promises and make of Abram a great nation. So, with trust that God would protect him, Abram went forth.

Like Abram, those of us who go forth carry with us a promise and a message. The promise is from the God who sends us forth. This sending forth reminds us that we are pilgrims on the earth; that we should never grow too attached to what belongs to the earth, as we are only passing through. The journey of life is one of constantly moving on to new lands of insight, holiness, and change.

The message that we as pilgrims carry with us is that God is the one who leads this ongoing migration. God calls all of us to live symbolically in tents rather than houses. A house represents stability — no change, no conversion. A tent represents a restlessness, a searching for that which really matters. By bringing this message to the world, we may remind others of the universal pilgrim status of all peoples.

Meditation: In what area of your life have you built a house instead of a tent?

Prayer: God of Abram, you called this great patriarch to leave his homeland and to journey to a new land that you would show him. You promised that you would make of him a great nation and that you would always be with him. Never let us forget our pilgrim status. Continue to pour out your blessing upon us as we make your journey through this life to the eternal life that you have promised through Jesus Christ, your Son, who lives and reigns with you and the Holy Spirit, one God, forever and ever. Amen.

Activity: Make a list of three ways in which you have been sent forth in the past. Make a list of three ways in which you think God may be sending you forth right now. Are you ready to travel?

Cycle B

AGENDA

Scripture: God put Abraham to the test. He called to him, "Abraham!" "Ready!" he replied. Then God said: "Take your son Isaac, your only one, whom you love, and go to the land of Moriah. There you shall offer him up as a holocaust on a height that I will point out to you."   (Genesis 22:1-2)

Mass: Genesis 22:1-2, 9, 10-13, 15-18; Romans 8:31-34; Mark 9:2-10

Reflection: There are a lot of things that are precious in a person's life. It might be a husband, a wife, child, a pet, or an object that has many memories associated with it. Looking around a person's home will almost always reveal a variety of precious people and things.

What is held as precious is also priceless. The person has no equal. The object cannot be bought or sold. An identical object would not be the same; it cannot be replaced. What is precious reveals a promise of the future. What is precious may recall past experiences, but that named precious also points toward the future.

Abraham's promise was a son, Isaac. God had promised a son in Abraham's and Sarah's old age, and he was born. In this

one boy was crystallized the hope, the promise, and the future
for Abraham's tribe, his people. How stunned he must have been
when he heard God instructing him to take his hope, his
promise, his future — his son — and make a sacrificial holocaust
of him!

Abraham learned what is easy to forget: what is precious
must often give way to what is more precious. This is not an easy
lesson for anyone to learn, because it involves sacrifice. God was
not interested in a human sacrifice; God was interested in the
sacrifice of Abraham's agenda. Once God convinced Abraham
that God had everything under control, then Abraham would
trust more, believe more, and get out of the way more. Today,
more than ever, people place their own personal, precious
agenda — which contains promises, hopes, and future plans —
before God's agenda, God's will. It's easier this way. But God has
no way to work out his will in a person's life as long as that person
continues to insist on his or her own way.

Abraham learned what every human being must ultimately
learn: what is precious in human eyes is not necessarily what
God considers percious. God calls people to abandon their
precious people and precious things. Once these are freely given
away, then God's will is made known. After this, what is
precious to God is given back. Abraham got back Isaac only after
he was willing to give him away.

Meditation: What precious person or thing keeps you from
permitting God to work his will in your life?

Prayer: God of Abraham, you called your servant to take the
son he loved, to go to a place that you would show him, and to
offer him as a sacrifice. Abraham was found obedient to your
will; he was willing to give away what he considered precious in

order to do your will. Do not put us to the test, but guide our hearts to understand what really matters in your sight. Give us the strength to remove whatever keeps us from doing your will. We ask this through our Lord Jesus Christ, your Son, who lives and reigns with you and the Holy Spirit, one God, forever and ever. Amen.

Activity: List three precious people or things. How have you had to be able to give these away in order to receive them back full of hope and promise for the future? How has God used them to bring about his will in your life?

Cycle C

PRESENCE

Scripture: The Lord God answered Abram, "Bring me a three-year-old heifer, a three-year-old she-goat, a three-year-old ram, a turtledove and a young pigeon." He brought him all these, split them in two, and placed each half opposite the other; but the birds he did not cut up. When the sun had set and it was dark, there appeared a smoking brazier and a flaming torch, which passed between those pieces. It was on that occasion that the LORD made a covenant with Abram.   (Genesis 15:9-10, 17-18)

Mass: Genesis 15:5-12, 17-18; Philippians 3:17-4:1; Luke 9:28-36

Reflection: If we listen carefully, we can often hear individuals say, "Someone is watching out for him." After coming close to an accident, we may overhear someone say, "Thank God no one was hurt!" After the death of a loved one, who may have really struggled, we may hear, "Now, she is at peace."

What do all these comments mean? What, one wonders, is behind them?

Most of the time such comments reveal a person's faith in God. The comments function as flashing neon lights; they herald signs of God's presence. One doesn't have to use the word "God" in order to indicate God's presence. One doesn't have to use a religious object to draw attention to him. If listened to carefully, people are identifying the presence of God in their lives all the time in diverse and multiple ways.

The recognition of God's presence is referred to as a "theophany" in religious literature. A theophany is a manifestation of God. Since no word or object can adequately convey the presence of God, human beings choose those signs which attempt to identify the Divine who is beyond all identification.

The author of Genesis used the number "3" to indicate the presence of God to Abram. The patriarch was instructed to bring three three-year-old animals to prepare for the covenant-making ceremony. Three alone signifies ritual maturity, but three sets of three signifies the divine presence. The author is shouting, "God is here!"

The revelation of the presence of God continues in other signs. The smoking brazier and the flaming torch function as indicators of God's presence. Throughout the Hebrew Scriptures, smoke and fire are signs of divine intervention in history. God enters into covenant with Abram. By passing through the split animals, both God and Abram declare that if either of them breaks the covenant that what happened to the animals will happen to them. In other words, God and Abram "cut a covenant."

The signs which indicated the divine presence in the past have given way to new and different signs today. It takes the observant person, the one who watches carefully and listens attentively, to recognize them.

 Meditation: What was the most recent sign of God's activity in your life?

Prayer: God of Abram, you brought your patriarch from his own country to a new land. You promised him that his descendants would be as numerous as the stars in the sky or the sand on the seashore. You revealed your presence to him in sacred numbers and smoke and fire. You have brought us to the new land of eternal life through the suffering, death, and resurrection of your Son, Jesus. Do not forget the promises that you have made to us. Help us to recognize the signs of your presence today. We ask this through our Lord Jesus Christ, who lives and reigns with you and the Holy Spirit, one God, forever and ever. Amen.

Activity: Make a list of the signs of God's presence in your life during the past week.

REBELLION

Scripture: Daniel prayed "Ah, Lord, great and awesome God, you who keep your merciful covenant toward those who love you and observe your commandments! We have sinned, been wicked and done evil; we have rebelled and departed from your commandments and your laws."

(Daniel 9:4-5)

Mass: Daniel 9:4-10; Luke 6:36-38

Reflection: When we hear the word "rebellion," we may automatically think of a revolution, the overthrow of a government. Or we might understand rebellion as a peaceful demonstration, within which people show their unity in opposition to a political or moral issue. A rebellion can also mean non-violent defiance of, or resistance to, authority — legal, ecclesial, moral. Of course, the one who participates in any type of rebellion is known as a rebel.

In the spiritual sphere, one can rebel against God. In this case, rebellion is known as sin — an attempt to take over the role of God and act like gods. Spiritual rebellion happens after a person carefully discerns the will of God, has a good idea what God wants, and proceeds to follow a different course. Spiritual rebellion takes place when, in a moment of crisis, one despairs and quits praying and says, "Prayer doesn't do any good anyway!"

Refusing to join the community of believers for worship can be spiritual rebellion. Either because one sees his or her fellow worshipers as hypocrites or because one thinks that worship is for those who have never truly grown into full adulthood, such an abandonment of the community is, nevertheless, a spiritual rebellion.

God permits spiritual rebellions because these allow people to be stretched; growth takes place during a period of rebellion. One person may learn how to do God's will more carefully. Another may learn the authentic power of prayer. Still another may come to acknowledge the importance of the Christian community. Because of God's great compassion and forgiveness, God does not squash any rebellion. Rather, God waits for the rebels to return shamefaced. Then, he accepts them back with mercy and with love.

Meditation: What was your most recent spiritual rebellion?

Prayer: Great and awesome God, you never forget your covenant with your people. We are sinners, who often rebel against your commandments and your laws. We do not always listen to your servants, the prophets, nor to your Son, our Lord Jesus Christ. We rely upon your compassion and forgiveness as we return to you. Help us to learn from our rebellious ways. Grant us your mercy and love through our Lord Jesus Christ, who lives and reigns with you and the Holy Spirit, one God, forever and ever. Amen.

Activity: Identify the last three great spiritual rebellions that have taken place in your life. What truth did you learn from each? Who or what prompted you to return to God's ways?

SIN

Scripture: Come now, let us set things right,
  says the LORD:
Though your sins be like scarlet,
  they may become white as snow;
Though they be crimson red,
  they may become white as wool.

(Isaiah 1:18)

Mass: Isaiah 1:10, 16-20; Matthew 23:1-12

Reflection: If asked to define sin, many people will say that it is something that is thought, said, or done which was contrary to the will of God. A few might add that sin can also be something that is omitted — something that should have been thought, said, or done but wasn't.

From this understanding there emerge various images of sin. Some might look at others and think themeselves superior because of their skin color, economic status or style of clothes. During a break at work, someone might tell everything that he or she had learned about a fellow employee. A husband cheats on his wife, or a wife on her husband. A parent abuses a child, or a child refuses to obey the family rules. Someone knows of a case of child abuse but never reports it to authorities. An accident is witnessed but the person drives on by.

Different people will draw different conclusions concerning the gravity of the list of sins presented above. However, it would be hard to argue that there was no sin involved. Sin, if looked at carefully, can be seen as that which separates a person from the human community and from God. In other words, sin has a communal dimension as well as an individual and personal one.

Through the prophet Isaiah, God calls the community to turn from sin. By turning away from sin — reforming — the people would also find themselves turning toward each other and God. In God's eyes, there is no sin which cannot be remitted. Even if the color of one's sin is scarlet — deadly — repentance can bleach it so that it becomes white again.

Meditation: What sin of commission or omission do you need to bring to your community of faith and to God so that it can be bleached?

Prayer: Lord God, you call your people to wash themselves clean by putting away their misdeeds and by ceasing to do evil. Through the community of believers you issue your call of repentance. Guide the process of our Lenten reform. We trust that our scarlet sins will become white as wool in your sight. Hear us as we pray through our Lord Jesus Christ, your Son, who lives and reigns with you and the Holy Spirit, one God, forever and ever. Amen.

Activity: Make a list of the sins with which you find you struggle most. What is the color of each sin? Explain your choice of color. What action could you initiate which might help you to begin to reform?

PLOTS

Scripture: "Come," they said, "let us contrive a plot against
Jeremiah. It will not mean the loss of instruction
from the priests, nor of counsel from the wise, nor of
messages from the prophets."   (Jeremiah 18:18)

Mass: Jeremiah 18:18-20; Matthew 20:17-28

Reflection: Usually a plot is a secret plan which is set in motion
in order to accomplish an evil deed. The villain's plan to defeat
the poor widow is a plot. The bank robber's plan to hold up the
teller is a plot. In a novel, the confrontation of the bad guys with
the hero or heroine (the good guy) is a plot. Any evil scheme
which tries to thwart a good deed is matter for a plot.

Although reluctant to admit it, many people spend much
of their lives plotting. One person spends hours carefully
calculating every penny in an effort to avoid paying even the
minutest amount of income tax. Some cut their taxes short and
later are investigated by the IRS! Such a plot is often foiled.

A plot is often uncovered at the work place. Employees
work harder when the boss is around than when he or she is
gone. They calculate how much work needs to be done in order
to avoid recriminations. They plan how to take off a few extra
hours, an extended lunch or coffee break, an extra thirty minutes
spent shopping after a dental appointment, an unexcused sick
day off. These are plots.

Even one's relationship with God can become part of a plot. People attend Mass every Sunday — not because they want to praise God but out of pure obligation, fearing the loss of their eternal salvation if they don't comply with the rule. Every action is weighed against the commandments in order to get by with as much as one can without making God too unhappy. A sizeable contribution to the Church can often serve as a "bribe" to complete the plan.

Doing the right thing for the wrong reason is bad. God is not a power to be appeased. God wants a genuine, trusting and trustful relationship with those who worship him out of love, obey him because it is the right thing to do, and contribute because they want to share their wealth with others. Instead of a plot, God is interested in a mature spiritual relationship with us as adults.

Meditation: Is your friendship with God a plot or an adult relationship?

Prayer: Lord, heed us and listen to what our adversaries say against us. Protect us from the plots of others and from the ones we unwittingly enter into ourselves. Help us to stand before you and to speak your words of truth. Give us the right motivation that we might enter into a trusting relationship with you, who live and reign with your Son, our Lord Jesus Christ, and your Holy Spirit, one God, forever and ever. Amen.

Activity: Make a list of three plots in which you have found yourself involved at home, at work, at school, at play, or with God. What do you need to do in order to stop plotting and to begin to live the truth?

FAITH

Scripture: Cursed is the man [or woman] who trusts
          in human beings,
          who seeks his [or her] strength in flesh,
          whose heart turns away from the LORD.
        He [or she] is like a barren bush in the desert
          that enjoys no change of season . . .
        Blessed is the man [or woman] who trusts in the
          LORD,
          whose hope is the LORD.
        He [or she] is like a tree planted beside the waters
          that stretches out its roots to the stream.
                                                        (Jeremiah 17:5-8)

Mass: Jeremiah 17:5-10; Luke 16:19-31

Reflection: When we trust someone else, we place our confidence in that person. We possesses an assured reliance on the character, ability, strength, and truth of that individual. A person who becomes willingly dependent upon another is said to trust the other. Such a trust is faith, a confident assurance grounded in hope that the other will do or say what he or she promises to do or say and will not disappoint.

   This type of trust in human beings is a glimpse of what authentic faith in God is all about. If we can taste the trust of a fellow human being, then we are simultaneously beginning to come to a true faith in God. At this point in our life, we may feel like a barren bush. There are no outer signs of the life of faith.

Interiorly, we resemble a desert or a lava waste and feel quite empty. Nothing seems to be growing; all is at a standstill. Faith in human beings must move us to trust in God.

To trust God means that we are willing to go out on a limb. Such blind faith, though not unreasonable, is not based on empirical factors. When we trust God, we simply trust God. The moment such faith is declared is the same moment that we begin to feel like a tree planted near a running stream. We are refreshed and realize that all does not depend upon us alone, but upon God. Faith becomes like roots, which soak up the flowing waters of God's grace until our whole being blossoms with life.

Everything else around us may begin to fall apart, but even in such a dry time trust prohibits distress or despair. Life continues to flourish and to bear the fruit of good works. Such faith can sustain us through any trial or crisis.

Meditation: When did you last put more trust in human beings than in God? What were the results? When did you last put more trust in God than in human beings? What were the results?

Prayer: Lord, you probe the mind and you test the heart. You offer your gift of trust to every person. Teach us through our trust of others to trust you even more. Keep us from becoming like barren bushes in the desert. Make us like trees planted beside flowing streams that we might drink of the grace of your Holy Spirit, who lives and reigns with you and your Son, our Lord Jesus Christ, one God, forever and ever. Amen.

Activity: Over the past five years through which experiences have you discovered that you were planted in the desert, and through which experiences have you learned that you were planted beside cool waters? What have you learned from each of these experiences?

UNEQUAL LOVE

Scripture: Israel loved Joseph best of all his sons, for he was the child of his old age; and he had made him a long tunic. When his brothers saw that their father loved him best of all his sons, they hated him so much that they would not even greet him.   (Genesis 37:3-4)

Mass: Genesis 37:3-4, 12-13, 17-28; Matthew 21:33-43, 45-46

Reflection: In theory, almost everything in the United States is based on a principle of equality. Every person is equal to every other person — no matter what one's ethnic background might be or what color of skin one might have. Everyone has the right to a trial by jury, for example. Everyone is entitled to an education. The list of equalities is endless.

From this basic principle there emerges an often unspoken presupposition that every mother and father loves each one of their children equally. Some parents attempt to demonstrate this by being very careful not to give gifts which are of unequal value to their children. Therefore, if Johnny gets a pair of pants for his birthday — valued at $40 — then Suzzie must get a dress for her birthday — valued at $40. Otherwise, the parents might be accused of loving the one more than the other.

Obviously there is something wrong here. Every person is unique. It is impossible to love everyone in just the same way. One cannot love all people equally. Only God can do that. And if

God's love is viewed from the perspective of the various gifts given to each person, then it might be true to say that even God doesn't love everyone equally. He does, however, love each one impartially and unconditionally.

The love of a husband and wife for each other is not the same as the love that each of them has for their parents and special friends. Mothers and fathers do not love each of their children in exactly the same way. Children do not love their parents in equal ways. Some children prefer to spend more time with one parent than with the other. This doesn't mean that they don't love the other parent with whom less time is spent. It just means that the love is different. To pretend otherwise is to risk a lot of misunderstanding, stress and, eventually, the authentic truth.

Once the fact that people do not love each other in the same way is faced, then the authentic love that does exist can be cultivated. We do not love someone more or less in comparison to another person. We simply love another. The way this love is expressed will vary according to the love relationship.

In the case of children, there may be moments of anger and jealousy as children learn that all love relationships are not equal. However, isn't it better to teach children that they are each loved in a special way, but not alike, than to teach them that they are all loved equally, a feat which no one can accomplish?

Meditation: In which way have you most recently expressed your love for your father, mother, brothers, sisters, children, uncles, aunts, friends, etc.?

Prayer: God of Israel and Joseph, you never forget your people, but you hold them in the palm of your hand. Israel, your patriarch, loved all twelve of his sons, but he loved Joseph best of all. Help us to understand the mystery of love. Keep us from making our love for others an equation. Make our love free and genuine like the love shared between you, Father, and your Son, our Lord Jesus Christ, and your Holy Spirit, who live and reign as one God, forever and ever. Amen.

Activity: Make a list of the people you love. In what special way do you love each of them?

FORGIVENESS

Scripture: Who is there like you, the God who removes guilt
                and pardons sin for the remnant of his inheritance;
              Who does not persist in anger forever,
                but delights rather in clemency,
              And will again have compassion on us,
                treading underfoot our guilt?
              You will cast into the depths of the sea all our sins.

(Micah 7:18-19)

Mass: Micah 7:14-15, 18-20; Luke 15:1-3, 11-32

Reflection: Every one of us has experienced anger at one time
or another in our life. A man may have gotten angry with himself
because he couldn't master carpentry. A woman may have
gotten angry with the vacuum cleaner when it refused to remove
the dirt from the floor. Children get angry with their toys and
throw them down or step on them.

We also get angry with each other. We may get angry with
the boss at work for failing to understand our new idea. After
getting delayed in traffic, we get home to discover that our
spouse is upset because we're late. A child gets angry with
another child who confiscates a toy.

Because of these types of experiences with anger, we've also
experienced pardon or forgiveness. No one can persist in anger
forever, although some people have been known to hold grudges
for years. When we're able to forgive ourself for not being able to

master every wood-working technique in the world, we experience the removal of guilt. When marriage partners are able to
say to each other, "I'm sorry," they experience each other's
pardon. Even children can be taught clemency, as they freely
offer the toy to the one who wanted to confiscate it to begin with.

Through these experiences of anger and consequent forgiveness, we are able to begin to get a glimpse of the compassion
of God. God removes guilt, pardons sin, and delights in clemency. He casts our sin into the depths of the sea. If God were
asked to remember what he had just forgiven, he wouldn't be
able to call those sins to mind. In other words, God's forgiveness
is unlimited.

Just as God cannot persist in anger, so we should never
hold grudges. The experience of anger should lead to an expression of pardon. It is through human experiences that God
permits us a glimpse of divine compassion.

Meditation: With whom were you most recently angry and
experienced the power of forgiveness?

Prayer: Lord God, there is no one like you, who removes guilt
and pardons sin. You take delight in clemency and compassion.
You cast our sins into the depths of the sea. Lead us through our
experiences of anger to the joy of forgiveness. Help us to
recognize your presence every time we reach out in love to
another. We ask this though our Lord Jesus Christ, your Son,
who lives and reigns with you and the Holy Spirit, one God,
forever and ever. Amen.

Activity: Make a list of people with whom you have been angry
during the past year. How have you experienced forgiveness
from, and offered pardon to, each of them?

Cycle A

GRUMBLING

Scripture: In their thirst for water, the people grumbled against Moses, saying, "Why did you ever make us leave Egypt? Was it just to have us die here of thirst with our children and our livestock?" (Exodus 17:3)

Mass: Exodus 17:3-7; Romans 5:1-2, 5-8; John 4:5-42

Reflection: When people don't get enough sleep, they are grumpy the next day. When they don't get enough food to eat, they are grouchy. When there is insufficient water to drink, they grumble. Besides these three basic physical necessities, clothing and shelter could also be added. "I don't have a thing to wear," or "It's too hot in here, or too cold" are common complaints we've all heard time and time again.

Grumbling signifies human displeasure. When one person complains about another, there exists some insufficiency which needs to be provided. A couple more hours of sleep might take care of the problem. Another hamburger might be the solution or a glass of diet soda. Maybe a slight adjustment on the thermostat will stop the grumbling.

If examined carefully, however, every complaint has hidden within itself its own solution. In other words, the only person who can bring it to an end is the individual who is doing the complaining. While it is true that some people live on grumbling, most can erase their dissatisfaction. Usually all it takes is for someone to come along with a staff of understanding and strike the heart of the problem. People get so caught up in their own grumbling that often they are not even aware that they're complaining and, consequently, they can't begin to put their finger on the hidden problem. So it takes another person to help them pin point the real reason behind it.

Sometimes this can be done very simply. When someone is grumpy, ask him or her about last night's sleep. If the response is, "I didn't sleep well at all last night; I tossed and turned the whole time," then perhaps a nap or an earlier bedtime tonight might be in order. If insufficient food and drink is the culprit, perhaps a bigger breakfast or a light snack might be the answer. If someone is complaining about the heat or cold, investigate the thermostat. Most of the time, a simple adjustment in the physical environment can do wonders for the psychological environment as well. Other solutions might entail either putting on or taking off a sweater.

The important thing is that someone listen, understand, and care. It's amazing how often grumbling ceases once the real source is identified and dealt with.

Meditation: What did you most recently grumble about? What was the solution to your problem?

Prayer: God of Moses, in the desert your people grumbled against your servant, Moses, because they had no water to drink. In your infinite wisdom, you instructed Moses to strike the rock and water would flow from it for the people to drink. We are a people who often grumble. Send us a prophet like Moses who will understand our problems and offer us solutions. Enable us to drink of the grace of your Son, Jesus, who lives and reigns with you and the Holy Spirit, one God, forever and ever. Amen.

Activity: Make a list of the three most frequent complaints that you have. Beside each list ways that you can solve your grumbling about each of these problems.

Cycle B

JEALOUSY

Scripture: "I, the LORD, am your God, who brought you out
of the land of Egypt, that place of slavery. . . . I, the
LORD, your God, am a jealous God."

(Exodus 20:2, 5)

Mass: Exodus 20:2-17; 1 Corinthians 1:22-25; John 2:13-25

Reflection: A person who is jealous is one who cannot tolerate
rivalry or unfaithfulness. Such a one is usually hostile toward a
rival or another who, for whatever reason, is believed to have
some advantage. The jealous person keeps vigil and guards what
he or she believes to belong to him or her.

Jealousy frequently manifests itself between those who are
dating or "going steady." Such a couple cannot tolerate the
thought that another person might want to date one or the other
of them. If the man finds the woman showing any form of
affection to another man, he suspects unfaithfulness. If the
woman observes the man spending too much time with another
woman, she may become hostile to the other woman. Such
jealousy is witnessed frequently in high schools where young
people seem to fall in and out of love every day.

Jealousy, though, can be found also in child-parent relationships. How often does one child become jealous of what his
or her sibling has received from one of the parents? It might be a

gift, some extra time spent on homework, or some special care demonstrated during an illness. Whatever the occasion, the one child becomes jealous of the attention received by the other.

Adults are not immune from jealousy. They go to great lengths to protect that which they consider especially valuable. The more precious the item, the more securely it is locked up. Safes, locked curio cabinets, and doors with dead-bolts indicate just how jealously the contents of the house are guarded.

God is jealous. It is difficult to predicate jealousy of God, but God does not tolerate rivalry or unfaithfulness. All of us are equally precious to God. He vigilantly guards us all because he has chosen us to be his own. This "jealous" God delivers us from slavery — physically, emotionally, mentally, and spiritually — and invites us to offer our allegiance to him alone.

Meditation: In which most recent way do you think that God has demonstrated his jealousy for you?

Prayer: Jealous God, once you led your chosen people from Egyptian slavery to a land flowing with milk, honey and freedom. You gave them your commandments that in keeping them they might demonstrate their faithfulness to your covenant. Give us the strength to keep your laws and to do your will. May we always remain faithful to you, Father, Son, and Holy Spirit, one God, living and reigning forever and ever. Amen.

Activity: Make a list of three people who have triggered jealousy in you. For each one identify the ways in which you expressed this jealousy. How were you able to get over your jealous feelings?

Cycle C

SACRED PLACES

Scripture: Leading the flock across the desert, [Moses] came to
Horeb, the mountain of God. There an angel of the
LORD appeared to him in fire flaming out of a
bush. God said, "Come no nearer! Remove the
sandals from your feet, for the place where you
stand is holy ground. I am the God of your father,"
he continued, "the God of Abraham, the God of
Isaac, the God of Jacob." "I am who am."

(Exodus 3:1-2, 5-6, 14)

Mass: Exodus 3:1-8, 13-15; 1 Corinthians 10:1-6, 10-12;
Luke 13:1-9

Reflection: Every religion has one or more sacred places —
locations where the divine is said to live or where the divine can
be found. Stonehenge, on Salisbury Plain in England, is one such
sacred place. The Wailing Wall in Jerusalem is a sacred place for
the Jews. Moslems hold that the rock from which Mohammed is
said to have ascended into heaven is a sacred place. For Catholics, the basilica of St. Peter in Rome is such a spot. The
Anglicans have their Canterbury Cathedral. Churches, syna-
gogues, mosques, groves, streams, and mountains are con-

sidered to be places where God — Yahweh, Allah, Jesus, or whatever other name one gives to God — can be found.

Besides these types of sacred places, every person has some location that is held in high esteem because of its relationship to the divine. For one it might be a mountaintop experience; a climb to the summit of a mountain to listen to the silence there may trigger the memory of a personal encounter with God. Another person may think of the ocean as a place where an encounter with the divine took place. The rhythm of the sea, the steady pounding of the surf, the gentle lapping of the water on the shore can spark memories of past experiences of the presence of God.

A person's home can also be a sacred place. The exact location might be a particular room, a prayer corner, a certain window. The individual returns to one of these spots over and over again in order to renew his or her contact with the divine. Such locations can be considered holy ground, places where one's shoes are symbolically removed and one reverently approaches God.

Whenever contact with the divine is made, everyone's immediate response is to name the experience. People want to know God's name; it is a human desire to know God, to be able to speak with him and about him. So different groups of people call God in various ways and by various names. Yet no single name can capture the essence of one's experience of God. For this reason, people return time and time again to these sacred places.

Meditation: Where is your sacred place? What happened there and when? How often do you frequent it?

Prayer: God of Abraham and Sarah, Isaac and Rebekah, Jacob and Leah, Rachel, Bilhah, and Zilpah, you revealed your presence to your servant, Moses, in a burning bush on Mount Horeb where you also revealed your name to him. Today, guide our feet to your holy places that we might recognize your presence with us. Father, still our hearts, quieten our spirits, and open our eyes to the revelation of the love you share with your Son, our Lord Jesus Christ, who lives and reigns with you and the Holy Spirit, one God, forever and ever. Amen.

Activity: Make a list of three to five sacred places that you have discovered in your life. After each indicate what revelation you received or what lesson you learned or what insight you attained there.

QUARRELING

Scripture: The place was called Massah and Meribah, because the Israelites quarreled there and tested the LORD, saying, "Is the LORD in our midst or not?"

(Exodus 17:7)

Mass: Exodus 17:1-7; John 4:5-42

Reflection: The name "Massah" means "the place of the test," and the word "Meribah" means "the place of the quarreling." After Moses led the Israelites from Egyptian slavery to desert freedom, they began to quarrel with him because they were thirsty and wanted water to drink. They had seen all the signs that God had worked in the land of Egypt but, nevertheless, they tested God; they wanted to know if the Lord was with them or not.

It is easy to determine the presence of another person. One can see the other sitting in the same room or standing near a window or walking through a door. One knows that the other is present. Some people have a sense of the presence of another person. The other may not be seen, but some type of intuition leads one to "know" that another is present or to "feel" the other's presence.

When a person is absent, a photograph is often displayed as a reminder of the presence of that individual somewhere in the world of the living or the dead. Paintings of mountains and oceans and farms are placed on walls as reminders of the presence of their beauty.

How does a person discern the presence of God? In the words of the Israelites, "Is the LORD in our midst or not?" (Exodus 17:7). There is no bodily presence, as if God would sit in a chair at the dining room table or walk through the door. There is no photograph of God that can be displayed on one's dressing table or book shelf. Paintings of mountains, oceans, and farms are not pictures of God.

After a moment's thought, it suddenly dawns upon one that Massah and Meribah are names of places that every person inhabits. Each one of us puts God to the test and asks the question about presence. Each one of us quarrels with God from time to time. Ask the individual who has cancer if she has ever questioned the presence of God in her life. Be ready for a hearty "Yes."

Ask the parents of a six-year-old child who died because he could not get a liver transplant if they ever questioned the presence of God. Ask them if they quarreled with God after the death of their son. Again, be ready for a resounding "Yes."

The man who just lost his job because his place of work is going out of business will quarrel with God. Sooner or later he will ask, "If there really is a God, why is this happening to me?" Massah and Meribah name places that everyone has visited at one time or another in life.

Solutions and answers eventually come. The woman with cancer, the parents of the dead child, and the man with the lost job discover that grace begins to flow from the rock of their crisis as they reaffirm their faith and enter a new relationship with God. They find that the Lord is always in their midst.

Meditation: When did you most recently test God or quarrel with him? What was the problem? What was the solution?

Prayer: God of the Israelites, when your people tested you in the desert and questioned your presence, you instructed your servant, Moses, to strike the rock and to provide water for your thirsty people to drink. In our moments of crisis, make us aware of your constant care and presence in our lives. Forgive us for testing you or quarreling with you. We ask this through our Lord Jesus Christ, your Son, who lives and reigns with you and the Holy Spirit, one God, forever and ever. Amen.

Activity: Make a list of three times in your life when you doubted God's presence, that is, when you put God to the test or quarreled with him. After each, list the way that you came to know the caring presence of God again.

HEALING

Scripture: Naaman came with his horses and chariots and stopped at the door of Elisha's house. The prophet sent him the message: "Go and wash seven times in the Jordan, and your flesh will heal, and you will be clean." But Naaman went away angry, saying, "I thought that he would surely come out and stand there to invoke the LORD his God, and would move his hand over the spot, and thus cure the leprosy." . . . Naaman went down and plunged into the Jordan seven times at the word of the man of God. His flesh became again like the flesh of a little child, and he was clean.   (2 Kings 5:9-11, 14)

Mass: 2 Kings 5:1-15; Luke 4:24-30

Reflection: A person who has cancer wants to be healed. A person who has AIDS wants to be cured. Even the individual who is suffering from a common cold seeks healing.

The surgical removal of the tumor followed by chemotherapy is the usual procedure for healing cancer, insofar as one can speak of healing cancer. AIDS to this date has no cure; there are drugs which may cause a remission and some which give promise of a potential to heal, but nothing definitive has been found. Likewise, the common cold must simply run its course; over-the-counter drugs can remove many of the symptoms —

congested chest, runny nose, blocked sinuses, etc. — but there is no cure for the common cold.

Anyone who has ever been ill wants to be healed as soon as possible. The individual wishes that the doctor knew some magic formula which he could brew and give to the patient, or some incantation which he could chant, and an instantaneous cure would be the result. People seek healing because they do not like to suffer in either large or small degrees.

Sometimes the simplest cure (insofar as there may be a cure) is the most reliable. The best way to heal a person with cancer is to detect it early. The best way to avoid AIDS is to prevent its spread. An ounce of prevention, according to the old axiom, is better than a pound of cure. Almost every doctor tells the person suffering with the common cold to get plenty of rest, drink lots of liquids and, possibly, take an aspirin or aspirin substitute.

Diseases aren't the only things requiring a cure. Loneliness at times can be cured by a simple visit from a friend or a conversation on the phone. A broken heart can be mended through the care and understanding of a loved one. Prejudice can be cured by educating people to realize and appreciate the equal dignity of every human being.

Healing, if one notices carefully, most often takes place through the intervention of human beings. There are no magic brews or secret incantations. It seems that God has chosen to cure people through other people. Faith in the means he chooses to use is also helpful.

Meditation: With what illness have you most recently suffered? Who was instrumental in your cure? How did he or she help you?

Prayer: God of Elisha and Naaman, you sent your word of
healing to Elisha, your prophet, who delivered it to Naaman the
leper. At the word of the man of God, Naaman was healed.
Guide all people who spend their lives seeking cures for the
diseases which afflict your people. Be with doctors who prescribe
remedies for those who suffer. Be with nurses and those who
care for the ill. Enable those who are sick to see traced in their
lives the pattern of the paschal mystery of Jesus, your Son, who
lives and reigns with you and the Holy Spirit, one God, forever
and ever. Amen.

Activity: Make a list of the last three illnesses which you
suffered. Identify those who cared for you, who healed you, who
suffered along with you. How did you discover that the simplest
cure was the best healing?

PROMISES

Scripture: In the fire Azariah stood up and prayed aloud:
Do not take away your mercy from us,
　for the sake of Abraham, your beloved,
　Isaac your servant, and Israel your holy one,
To whom you promised to multiply their offspring
　like the stars of heaven,
　or the sand on the shore of the sea.

(Daniel 3:25, 35-36)

Mass: Daniel 3:25, 34-43; Matthew 18:21-35

Reflection: Every day people make promises to each other. Some of these are more binding or more serious than others. For example, a husband promises his wife that he will stop by the cleaners and pick up her coat. This promise is not as serious or as binding as those he made on the day of their wedding.

One child borrows a quarter from another child and promises to repay it the next day. This promise is not as serious or as binding as the promissory note an adult signs in order to get a loan to purchase a new home.

A friend on a trip promises to send a postcard or to call. Again, this promise is not as binding as a promise made to visit someone who is sick and needs constant care.

All of the human promises which are made in a day — some of which are kept and some of which are forgotten — cannot begin to measure up to the promises made by God. By solemn agreement God promised Abraham and Sarah that they would be the parents of a new people; they were to have descendants as countless as the stars in the sky or the sands along the seashore. God kept his promise, but his people often doubted and thought that they had to remind God of what he said.

In times of crisis, we often doubt the promise made to us by others. If it snows, will the one who promised to stop by every day continue to do so? Will the problems at work prohibit him from keeping his promise to be home early tonight? Will she have taken care of all the errands that she promised to run this morning even though the car broke down? It becomes hard to believe that someone will keep a promise when some type of crisis situation develops.

This is not true of God, however. God keeps the promises which he makes. His word is reliable. The need to remind God of his promises is not so much for God's sake as it is for ours. We need to remember that God is faithful.

Meditation: What promise did God most recently make to you and keep?

Prayer: God of Abraham and Sarah, Isaac and Rebekah, Israel and Leah, Rachel, Bilhah, and Zilpah, remember your covenant with us and have mercy upon us. Raise up leaders after your own heart who will keep us faithful. With contrite hearts and humble spirits, let us be received by you. Strengthen our trust in you that we may never be put to shame. We ask this through our Lord Jesus Christ, your Son, who lives and reigns with you and the Holy Spirit, one God, forever and ever. Amen.

Activity: Make a list of three promises you most recently made. Which of these did you keep? Which of them did you break? Why? Make a list of three promises others made to you. Which of these did they keep? Which of these did they break? Do you know why?

LAWS

Scripture: "I teach you the statutes and decrees as the LORD, my God, has commanded me, that you may observe them in the land you are entering to occupy. Observe them carefully, for thus will you give evidence of your wisdom and intelligence to the nations, who will hear of all these statutes and say, 'This great nation is truly a wise and intelligent people.' For what great nation is there that has gods so close to it as the LORD, our God, is to us whenever we call upon him?"   (Deuteronomy 4:5-7)

Mass: Deuteronomy 4:1, 5-9; Matthew 5:17-19

Reflection: In the midst of trying to keep the law — social, public, ecclesial, moral, etc. — we often forget that the law exists to protect us. Highway laws are enacted in order to keep persons operating motor vehicles — cars, vans, trucks, buses, jeeps, etc. — from accidents and thus injuring or killing each other. However, if one is late for an appointment and in a hurry to get there as close to "on time" as possible, then the law that is designed to protect people can, seemingly, become a hindrance.

Parents promulgate laws for their children in order to protect their offspring. Curfews are set. Boundaries which indicate how far one can wander away from the neighborhood are drawn. With whom the child can play is clearly defined. From the child's perspective these rules are a hindrance which curtail his fun. He may even think that his parents are "out to make life miserable" for him. However, the family guidelines are only meant to protect them.

The Church sets guidelines for her members; this set of rules and regulations is called the Code of Canon Law. The Code of Canon Law is not meant to be an obstacle which is placed in the middle of a person's pilgrimage of faith but, rather, it is designed to protect people. Some, of course, find that adhering to sacramental preparation programs or observing fast and abstinence regulations is too tedious, and they cannot see how such laws are a help on the journey to the fullness of salvation.

Oftentimes, excuses are made or reasons given to people for keeping the law. The oldest one is this: It is good for you. Another is: When you get older you will see the wisdom in the law. Sometimes you hear that you ought to keep the law simply "because."

The author of the book of Deuteronomy portrays Moses as delivering a speech about fidelity to the law to the Israelites. The emphasis of Moses' speech is on the community dimension of the statutes and decrees which God has given to his people through his servant, Moses. It is important to notice that Moses is interested in the fact that God's law is meant to protect.

By adhering to God's law the Israelites will demonstrate their wisdom and intelligence; they will show other nations what a great nation God has made of them. Other peoples will see through the Israelites' keeping of the law that God has chosen them to be his special people. The nation of Israel will not be like other nations, who must appease their gods. The nation of Israel has a very special relationship with God. By keeping God's statutes and decrees, the Israelites demonstrate how close the Lord, their God, is to them.

Meditation: Which law do you find the most difficult to keep? Why? How is this law designed to protect people?

Prayer: Lord our God, you have established your statutes and decrees in order to protect your people. Give us a deep appreciation for your law. Help us to recognize how close you are to us and how much you care for us. Guide us with your Holy Spirit through our lifetime pilgrimage that we might enter into the promised land of heaven, where you live and reign with Jesus, your Son, and the Holy Spirit, one God, forever and ever. Amen.

Activity: Make a list of any three laws which you think are useless. What do you think was the intention of the lawmaker in each case? Who was the law designed to protect? How does the law foster the well-being of the community?

STIFF NECKS

Scripture: They have not obeyed me nor paid heed; they have stiffened their necks and done worse than their fathers. When you speak all these words to them, they will not listen to you either; when you call to them, they will not answer you.   (Jeremiah 7:26-27)

Mass: Jeremiah 7:23-28; Luke 11:14-23

Reflection: To most people a stiff neck is an unpleasant experience. Such a tightening of the muscles in the neck can be caused by sleeping in a crooked position on a pillow or receiving a sudden jolt in an automobile accident (commonly referred to as whip-lash) or by keeping your head bent over a desk or work table all day, thus producing a strain on the neck.

However, a stiff neck can also refer to stubbornness. Those who refuse to listen to the wisdom of another are said to be stiff-necked; that is, they won't turn their neck even to hear the wise words of advice of another. From time to time, most of us suffer from this type of stiff neck.

For example, a parent of one family tells the parents of another how to raise their children. The issue may concern sports, drugs, sex, playmates, curfew, etc. In most cases the parent being given the advice will develop a stiff neck.

In a hierarchical situation, those perched on the higher rungs of the ladder are known for their wisdom — that is why they are near the top of the ladder — while those near the bottom are supposed to "do what they are told." If one of these do-what-you're-told types attempts to show one of the hierarchy another method or a time-saving technique or an alternative way to make profits, he or she will most likely find that the top-of-the-ladder types have stiff necks.

In the case of the Church, some of her members have stiff necks. "Oh, I get to Mass when I can. I don't worry about making it every Sunday," says one. "Who pays any attention to all that stuff that the pope says?" asks another. "I don't listen to the homily; our priest doesn't know what he's talking about," states a third. "Jesus really didn't mean that we had to do all of that," can also be heard. When we refuse to budge in our own positions we risk getting a very stiff neck.

It seems that a stiff neck is one of the most easily communicable diseases. It is characterized by an inability to listen attentively to the words of another, especially to the words of God.

Meditation: When did you most recently come down with a stiff neck? What was the reason?

Prayer: God of Jeremiah, you sent your prophet to your people when they walked in the hardness of their hearts and turned their backs to you. Come and open our ears, minds, and hearts that we might hear your word of repentance, understand your call to conversion, and be moved to turn our faces to you and receive your compassion. Once again, be our God and make us your chosen people. We ask this through our Lord Jesus Christ, your Son, who lives and reigns with you and the Holy Spirit, one God, forever and ever. Amen.

Activity: Make a list of the three most serious cases of stiff neck that you have had in the last month. What was the remedy for your cure? Who was involved? What were the wise words to which you first failed to listen?

RETURN

Scripture: Return, O Israel, to the LORD, your God;
you have collapsed through your guilt.
Assyria will not save us,
nor shall we have horses to mount;
We shall say no more, "Our god,"
to the work of our hands. . . .
I will heal their defection,
I will love them freely;
for my wrath is turned away from them.

(Hosea 14:2, 4-5)

Mass: Hosea 14:2-10; Mark 12:28-34

Reflection: The word "return" is formed from the prefix "re,"
which means "back," and "turn," which, among its almost full
dictionary page of definitions, means to "move." Basically, then,
"return" means to "move back." Such a "moving back" implies
that we have changed directions and are no longer where we
once were.

This is true spatially. Most people leave their homes to go
to work, or school, or shopping, and then they return to their
homes; that is, they go or "move back" to their homes.

This is also true mentally. It is not difficult to catch people
sitting in one place while their minds are delighting in being
elsewhere. This phenomenon is referred to as daydreaming or

mind wandering. With a nudge to the shoulder or a loud shout, the daydreamer "returns" to his senses, to his or her true mental location.

Spiritually, we need to "return" to God. More often than not most of us do not consciously take leave of God. What usually happens is that we begin to trust more in ourselves or in other things than we do in God. It is not uncommon to hear it said, "If you want this done right, you must do it yourself." Such an attitude can easily and unconsciously seep into our relationship with God. Consequently, we tend to rely more upon ourselves than upon the Almighty.

Objects can become gods. The computer operator has become a symbol of the all-powerful in the world today. Likewise, the successful Wall Street broker or the president of a corporation represent power and status. The desire to have a share in such human power structures can easily become one's god. What an individual does with his or her hands, mind, or heart can easily become his or her god.

Therefore, it is necessary and important that one "return" to the source of all power — God. The individual is not God. The computer is not God. Success is not God. All human abilities pale in the presence of God. When we begin to recognize our place in the great scheme of things, we also begin to recognize the God who keeps everything together and running smoothly.

If we need to "return," that is, to "move back" to God then we must first acknowledge our guilt; that we have been away. We must also recognize and remove the gods of self and machines and success which we've created. With all of these out of the way, then our conversion can begin. Hindrances are removed. We can bask again in God's love which is freely offered to those who "return."

Meditation: Identify one way in which you need to "return" to God. How can you, with God's help, accomplish this?

Prayer: Lord our God, we have collapsed through our own guilt. We have substituted ourselves, our work, and our success for you. Give us the grace of true conversion that we may return to you and be healed of our defection. Once again pour out your love upon us and turn away your wrath. We ask this through our Lord Jesus Christ, your Son, who lives and reigns with you and the Holy Spirit, one God, forever and ever. Amen.

Activity: Make a list of the ways that you have turned away from God during the past month. Choose one of these which you sincerely wish to change. Identify how you were led astray. Tell how you can return.

DAWN

Scripture: "Let us know, let us strive to know the LORD;
as certain as the dawn is his coming,
and his judgment shines forth like the light of day!
He will come to us like the rain,
like spring rain that waters the earth."
What can I do with you, Ephraim?
What can I do with you, Judah?
Your piety is like a morning cloud,
like the dew that early passes away.

(Hosea 6:3-4)

Mass: Hosea 6:1-6; Luke 18:9-14

Reflection: Each morning people around the world arise before or after the dawn. Those who roll out of bed in the darkness of the early morning can often watch the first streaks of light break over the east. Those who climb out of bed after the sun has arisen know that sometime earlier the day began with a tiny streak of light shattering the darkness of the night.

A lesson can be learned from the daily rhythmic arrival of the dawn. This lesson is one upon which the Church focuses during the Advent and Christmas seasons — the coming of the Lord. Just as dawn is a reliable daily event, so is the coming of the Lord — in his word, in the sacraments, and in his people. His second coming at the end of time is a special coming of the Lord, one that is still waiting to take place.

But we find it hard to wait. We're used to making things happen, to getting things now: satellite communications with persons around the world, supersonic travel on the futuristic Concorde, few-second meals from our microwave ovens. Instead of watching patiently for the dawn of the Lord's second coming, many of us have given up the hope or forgotten about the possibility of such a future event at all.

Our faithfulness might be compared to the rosy orange-streaked clouds that paint the sky at dawn. For a moment the light dances on the puffy white clouds and variegates them with shades of red and orange. In a few moments, though, all the color is gone as the bright golden disk of the sun begins to peek over the eastern horizon.

Faithlessness can be compared to the dew. In the early morning hours, the dew covers the lawn and drips from the leaves of the trees. It takes just a few minutes for it to disappear once the warm sunshine touches that to which it clings. Such is the steadfastness of those who do not keep a lifetime vigil for the Lord's second coming. It is like the dew that passes away in the early hours of morning.

Keeping before our mind the possibility of the Lord's second coming motivates us to keep involved in the process of our conversion. Our life is a never-ending series of steps taken up the rungs of the ladder of change. God is always at work in our life, purifying our hearts, calling us to authentic love, encouraging us to know, love, and serve him better.

Meditation: Yesterday, how were you changed? Was there any connection between the change and your keeping vigil for the Lord's second coming?

Prayer: Lord God, you call us to return to you so that you might heal us and bind up the wounds caused by our lack of fidelity. Through your Holy Spirit, help us to know you. Make up whatever is lacking in our faith. Give us patience and keep us prepared for the second coming of your Son, our Lord Jesus Christ, who lives and reigns with you and the Holy Spirit, one God, forever and ever. Amen.

Activity: Make a list of three simple ways in which you can prepare for the Lord's coming every day. What changes will you have to make in your life in order to remain faithful to these vigils?

Cycle A

ANOINTING

Scripture: The LORD said, "There — anoint him, for this is he!" Then Samuel, with the horn of oil in hand, anointed him in the midst of his brothers; and from that day on, the spirit of the LORD rushed upon David.   (1 Samuel 16:12-13)

Mass: 1 Samuel 16:1, 6-7, 10-13; Ephesians 5:8-14; John 9:1-41

Reflection: It is not infrequent for a person who suffers from arthritis to apply an ointment or salve to the aching joint in order to bring about some relief. Similarly, when a child scrapes a knee or cuts a finger or bruises an elbow, the child's parent usually applies some type of ointment to the wound. Babies are routinely oiled and powdered, and athletes have ointment poured on them while their tired muscles are being rubbed and kneaded and massaged.

Many sacraments incorporate some type of anointing into their prescribed rituals. Before children are baptized, they are first anointed with the Oil of Catechumens as a sign of strengthening. In the process of the Rite of Christian Initiation of Adults (RCIA), persons preparing to celebrate baptism can be anointed with the Oil of Catechumens a number of times in order to strengthen their resolve to profess their faith in Jesus.

After baptism both children and adults are anointed on the head with the chrism, a sweet-smelling oil made by mixing balsam (or myrrh) and olive oil. In confirmation the one being confirmed is anointed on the forehead with chrism. The hands of a newly ordained priest are anointed with this oil, as well as the head of a newly ordained bishop. Even altars, when they are dedicated, are anointed with chrism oil.

When people are ill, the priest prays for them and anoints them with the Oil of the Sick. This anointing is for comfort and for healing.

Sacramental anointings — representing strengthening, healing, comforting, and empowerment — are signs of the presence of the Holy Spirit. In baptism one is strengthened and immersed into water and the Spirit. In confirmation one is sealed again with the Spirit of faith and fire. In holy orders one is empowered to lead the community in prayer and worship by the Holy Spirit. In the anointing of the sick, the Holy Spirit brings healing and comfort to those who are ill.

There are other times, however when a person is anointed by God. There may be no visible smearing of oil, but the individual knows that he or she has been touched by God in a special way. This may take place during a moment of prayer. It might come as an insight or solution to a long-thought-out problem. A time of relief after a period of anxiety can signal God's anointing. With a few minutes of quiet God can anoint us with his peace. During these and other times, God's Spirit rushes upon us and we experience his presence and are never the same again.

Meditation: When did God most recently anoint you with the Holy Spirit?

Prayer: God of Samuel and David, once you sent your prophet to Jesse of Bethlehem to anoint his son, David, as king of Israel. When Samuel opened the horn of oil and poured it upon David's head, your Holy Spirit rushed upon him. Send the same Spirit to us in order to strengthen, comfort, heal and empower us. Through the guidance of your Holy Spirit, help us to know your will and to do it in our lives. We ask this through our Lord Jesus Christ, your Son, who lives and reigns with you and the Holy Spirit, one God, forever and ever. Amen.

Activity: Make a list of three special times that God has anointed you since your life began. Which of these were anointings of strength, comfort, healing, and empowerment?

Cycle B

CORRECTIONS

Scripture: Early and often did the LORD, the God of their fathers, send his messengers to them, for he had compassion on his people and his dwelling place. But they mocked the messengers of God, despised his warnings, and scoffed at his prophets. . . . Then he brought up against them the king of the Chaldeans. . . . Those who escaped the sword he carried captive to Babylon, where they became his and his sons' servants until the kingdom of the Persians came to power. . . . The LORD inspired King Cyrus of Persia to issue this proclamation . . .: "Thus says Cyrus, king of Persia: 'All the kingdoms of the earth the LORD, the God of heaven, has given to me. . . . Whoever among you belongs to any part of his people, let him go up, and may his God be with him!' " (2 Chronicles 36:15-17, 20, 22-23)

Mass: 2 Chronicles 36:14-17, 19-23; Ephesians 2:4-10; John 3:14-21

Reflection: None of us wants to be corrected. A correction indicates that we are doing something wrong. Since most of us tend to think that we're almost always right, when someone comes along and attempts to correct us, it becomes a humiliating experience.

At table someone may point out to us that we're using the wrong fork or spoon. The one doing the correcting may think that he or she is helping. We feel put down, though, and somewhat humiliated in the presence of others.

In a crowd of employees, the boss may call us over and begin to talk to us in hushed tones. Others wonder what is going on, and they may easily conclude that some type of corrective measure is being taken. We know that everyone is staring at us and we're embarrassed. Children, especially teenagers, often feel put down by adults who seem to choose the most inopportune time to remind them to take out the trash, to put gas in the car, or to go to bed. They're embarrassed when their parents tell stories about their early childhood. From their perspective, these things are humiliating and should never be revealed.

None of us likes to hear warnings, but sometimes they're necessary and the one giving them doesn't have time to assess the situation and determine whether it's the best time or not. Because so much is at stake, we may need to be told on the spot to straighten up and fly right or face severe consequences.

Not using the right fork may make us the butt of snobbish comments on the part of others, not listening to what the boss has to say could cost us our job, disregarding our parents' admonitions could cause us to make a mistake that will haunt us all our lives. We'd hardly consider those who have corrected us as saviors, but they may very well have been. God often chooses the least likely candidates in human eyes to get his work accomplished. The one who corrects or warns another may be the very one who saves him or her.

Meditation: Who most recently corrected you in some way? How did you respond initially? Later, after thinking about it, from what did this person save you?

Prayer: God of Cyrus, king of Persia, you called this conqueror of your people to permit your chosen ones to return to Jerusalem and to rebuild your temple there. Early and often we have mocked your messengers, despised your warnings, and scoffed at your prophets. Send us leaders who are on fire with your word and filled with your Spirit. Bring us back to you. We ask this through our Lord Jesus Christ, your Son, who lives and reigns with you and the Holy Spirit, one God, forever and ever. Amen.

Activity: Make a list of threes time that you have been corrected by others in the past. Why did you need the correction? What did you learn from it? Was the person who corrected you unexpected? In which ways are you a better person because of this warning, correction, or simple word of advice?

Cycle C

PASSOVERS

Scripture: While the Israelites were encamped at Gilgal on the plains of Jericho, they celebrated the Passover on the evening of the fourteenth of the month. (Joshua 5:10)

Mass: Joshua 5:9, 10-12; 2 Corinthians 5:17-21; Luke 15:1-3, 11-32

Reflection: It is no accident that the author of the book of Joshua portrays the Israelites celebrating the Passover after crossing the Jordan River. The parallel is obvious. Just as Moses led the people out of Egyptian slavery by crossing through the Sea of Reeds after they had celebrated the Passover, so Joshua led the people into the promised land through the Jordan River and celebrated the Passover. Thus, Joshua is portrayed as a leader like Moses.

Historically, the Passover commemorates the passing over of the angel of death. The houses of the Israelites were spared the death of the first-born, whereas the houses of the Egyptians suffered the loss of the first-born. In other words, the people passed over from imminent death (both in slavery and the first-born) to the possibility of a new life. The passing over continues at the Sea of Reeds. Again, the Israelites face imminent death from Pharaoh and his army, but Moses raises his arms and the sea divides. Thus, Israel passes over to the possibility of life again. Even the column of fire, the guiding presence of God, passes over the Israelites at the sea in order to protect them from Pharaoh and his troops.

It is not difficult to see why early Christians quickly interpreted Jesus' death and resurrection in Passover terms. He, the new paschal lamb, faced death, but he passed over to life. God revealed his glory through the death and resurrection — the greatest Passover ever — of his own Son, Jesus.

Passovers continue today. Maybe they are not aware of it, but people are always passing over from death to life. For example, one man is in a terrible automobile accident, yet he walks away from the totaled car without a scratch. He will tell you that he saw his life pass before him. He passed over from imminent death to life.

A woman faces an inner struggle concerning what to do with her life now that her children are raised and off to college. Should she stay home? Should she go back to school? Should she get a full-time job? Should she get part-time work? Her worry becomes so intense that she dies in the heap of questions only to find the answer at her lowest moment. She has passed over to life.

Children, while playing with other children, relinquish a toy that they prefer; they pass over to a new understanding of what it means to share. A girl is moved to give to charity a few extra dollars that she saved for a special purpose; a passover has just taken place. The doctor tells a patient that he will have to change his lifestyle in order to prevent a heart attack. Once the initial panic subsides, the change begins and the person passes over from an old way of life to a new way of living.

All day, every day, we celebrate passover. It is not an elaborate celebration but, nevertheless, it is an authentic remembrance of a change which has taken place in our lives. It is a remembrance of that moment when we faced death and discovered life.

Meditation: When did you most recently pass over from death to life?

Prayer: Saving God, through Joshua, your servant, you led your chosen people across the Jordan River to the land flowing with milk and honey. Once across they remembered and celebrated your great signs at the Sea of Reeds and the many occasions when you led them through death to life. We have been baptized into the paschal mystery of Jesus, your Son, who passed over from death to life. Help us to recognize your constant care for us. Keep us from fear as we journey toward the promised land of the kingdom where you live and reign with Jesus and the Holy Spirit, one God, forever and ever. Amen.

Activity: Make a list of what you consider to be your three greatest passovers. What was the death you faced? What was the life your received? What was the lesson that you learned?

ENEMIES AND JUSTICE

Scripture: Rejoice not over me, O my enemy!
though I have fallen, I will arise;
though I sit in darkness, the LORD is my light.

(Micah 7:8)

Mass: Micah 7:7-9; John 9:1-41

Reflection: Almost everyone has had an enemy at one time or another. An enemy isn't necessarily someone with whom you do battle — as in a war. Your enemy might be the neighbor next door who doesn't believe in raking his leaves in the fall. You get upset because his leaves keep blowing over into your well-manicured yard. The negligent neighbor is labeled the enemy.

Maybe your boss is the enemy. The person we work for is often the target of our hostility. The boss has to be kept happy and appeased at all costs. Whatever he or she says is unquestioned and unquestionable. Everything has to be handled according to the orders given by the boss. This, of course, can work the other way around. Maybe you're the boss and your employee is making life a hell for you: never on time, careless in the way the work is performed, always criticizing and causing trouble. Bosses have been know to bear down on difficult employees in an effort to make them quit and seek work elsewhere. Both can become the other's worst enemy.

Even children have enemies. One child takes the toy that

another wants and a minor war breaks out. Sometimes one child will slap, kick, or bite another and accuse the other of cheating or stealing or being unfair.

Sometimes an enemy can cause one to fail or be defeated. The neighbor who permits his leaves to roam freely may very well triumph over the person who wants to keep them out of his yard. An employee might be so good at keeping the boss happy that the boss doesn't realize how that employee might, in other ways, be deceiving him. Or the boss might make things so difficult that the employee has no choice but to resign her position. One child might intimidate another to the point that the other runs away and hides.

But in the midst of the enemy's triumph, the defeated still have hope. Might does not make right, and justice is not based on power or prestige. God's justice is based on truth and is meted out to those who trust. "Who can sit in the darkness and wait for my light?" God asks.

When we learn to put things in their proper perspective we can see how true this is. It is by being upset about some inconsequential leaves that we may learn how unimportant a well-manicured lawn may well be in the grand scheme of things. Employees and bosses may learn to respect one another and come to realize, after the heat of the argument has passed, that there are different ways of doing things and that the old way is not always the best. Even children can learn that the darkness of defeat can be a prelude to making friends. The one with whom we struggled yesterday may be our strongest supporter today.

Contrary to popular belief, light shines *out* of the darkness — not in spite of it. God's justice shows forth from the darkness of defeat. Night is often the background needed to see clearly the light of the Lord.

Meditation: When did an enemy last triumph over you? What was the issue? How dark did things become? What light emerged as a result?

Prayer: God our Savior, you do not permit the enemy to rejoice over us when we have fallen and sit in the midst of darkness and despair. Rather, you send your Spirit of insight to enlighten us and to bring us hope for your justice. Do not abandon us, but be ever close. Continue to bring forth from the darkness of our lives the light of your justice. We ask this through our Lord Jesus Christ, your Son, who lives and reigns with you and the Holy Spirit, one God, forever and ever. Amen.

Activity: Make a list of the last three major defeats which you experienced in your life. For each of these identify the enemy, the darkness, the insight, and the new perspective on life which you received.

NEW

Scripture: Lo, I am about to create new heavens
                 and a new earth;
                 The things of the past shall not be remembered
                 or come to mind.   (Isaiah 65:17)

Mass: Isaiah 65:17-21; John 4:43-54

Reflection: People who survive the trials and tribulations of life
are drawn to that which is new or re-created. Most of us,
therefore — because we are survivors — live for and thrive on
getting or discovering something new.

Families look forward to the day when they can purchase
and move into a new house. The old place may be too small, so a
new home is planned. Later, when the children move away, the
parents may look around for a place for their retirement, an
apartment or condominium — something smaller but, nonetheless, something new.

This search for the new can manifest itself in what some
call a career change. After being part of an assembly line or a
member of the white collar crowd or having served in the armed
forces, a person will look for a different job. It might be in a
related profession, but oftentimes it means going back to school
and being retrained for something entirely new.

Explorers and discoverers are held in universal high esteem
because they are in the business of uncovering and experiment-

ing with that which is new. Christopher Columbus is hailed as the one who discovered the new world; George Washington is honored as the first to lead a new nation, a new democracy, a new economic and political system designed to protect individual human rights and provide all with an opportunity to have a say in this new form of government. Astronauts are the new explorers, traveling through space in search of new information about the cosmos, of which our earth is but a speck. Scientists are the new discoverers trying to unlock the secrets of life and health.

Knowing that a cure may be just around the corner, the research scientist continues testing. Convinced that world hunger can be eliminated, the agriculturist labors to find improved methods of food production. Even the teenager behind the fast food counter and the carry-out person patiently look forward to the day when they will have a promotion, a new job, and a better life.

There is one frontier that every person will have to face sooner or later — death. The God who created the original heavens and earth promises that he will create a new heavens and a new earth. Of it we only know that eye has not seen nor ear heard the marvels which lie in store for us in this new creation. The satisfaction we will enjoy will be so intense that nothing of the past, which calmed the desire for something new for a time, will be remembered. All the "newness" which we experienced during life will pale in comparison to the eternal "newness" that awaits us. While getting little tastes of it in our lifetime, we look forward in hope to that which is to come.

Meditation: What was your most recent experience of something new? How was your sense of hope revivified?

Prayer: God of the new, once you created the heavens and the earth, but you promised that you would re-create them. Through our daily experiences of the new, give us hope for your eternal newness. Dry our tears. Remove our fear of death. Help us to remember the freshness and fullness of the new life which you promise us through our Lord Jesus Christ, your Son, who lives and reigns with you and the Holy Spirit, one God, forever and ever. Amen.

Activity: Make a list of what you consider to be your three greatest lifetime experiences of newness. Record your feelings about each. If these are but tastes of the newness promised by God, how can remembering these experiences lessen your fear of death?

THE POSITIVE

Scripture: The water had risen so high it had become a river that could not be crossed except by swimming. Along the bank of the river I saw very many trees on both sides.   (Ezekiel 47:5, 7)

Mass: Ezekiel 47:1-9, 12; John 5:1-3, 5-16

Reflection: While many people frequently experience a lot of negative events in their lives, there are also many positive things that happen in a lifetime. It seems that we are often prone to emphasize the negative — the illness, the mistake, the crisis — rather than to highlight the positive. However, like the unpleasant situations which occur during a day, there are also very pleasing experiences which take place.

For example, getting up in the morning after a good night's sleep is a positive experience, although many never think to look at it as such. Your body's rested; your mind's alert; the excitement of living another day fills your perspective. The sunrise brings a smile to your face. The morning shower re-baptizes you and you're ready to begin again.

The crisis waiting at work is faced resolutely and the strategy works. You sit for awhile and think about all that could have gone wrong but didn't. Then you consider how everything turned our for the best. A lot was learned. A number of people were stretched and grew. Life is not so bad after all!

Even children experience the superabundance of the positive. They find it in school where they learn new and exciting things each day. They rush home in the afternoon to share their discoveries with their parents or sitters. They find it with each other as they share toys and games and suddenly discover that they are immersed in a world where all is good and worthy of trust. Their eyes sparkle as they understand and speak about an idea that was planted, sprouted, grew, and bore fruit in their own minds.

All of these positive experiences represent a return to that paradise where God's grace initially flowed superabundantly like water in a stream. Here and now people stand along the bank of the river of all the positive experiences of their lives, and they drink freely. Like trees, they grow and produce fruit. Hopefully, they recognize the source of these blessings — God, who is a river of life for all.

Meditation: What was your most recent positive experience, which was also an experience of God's grace?

Prayer: God of the waters, from your temple in heaven you send forth the streams of your grace to your people. You flood us with your life through the daily experiences of our lives. Make us aware of your great love for us. Help us to recognize your presence throughout our day. Enable us to produce abundant fruit from the stream of the life of grace you share with us. We ask this through our Lord Jesus Christ, your Son, who lives and reigns with you and the Holy Spirit, one God, forever and ever. Amen.

Activity: Make a list of what you consider to be the three most positive experiences of your life. For each of these indicate what you learned, how you grew, and what changes you made in your life as a result of the experience. How was God present in each of these experiences?

FORGETFULNESS

Scripture: Can a mother forget her infant,
      be without tenderness for the child of her womb?
      Even should she forget,
         I will never forget you.

                                                    (Isaiah 49:15)

Mass: Isaiah 49:8-15; John 5:17-30

Reflection: We have a tendency to think of forgetfulness as just another aspect of the aging process. But, if we're honest, we find that we all forget something or other almost every day. "I forgot to pick up the dry cleaning." "I forgot to stop by the bank and deposit that check." "I couldn't for the life of me think of her name." "I forgot all about doing my homework last night."

In the workplace, forgetfulness can cost money. A worker who forgets to install a single bolt or screw or rivet in a new car on an assembly line can unwittingly set the company up for a huge lawsuit. A secretary who forgets to prepare a letter can lose large advertising income for a firm. Likewise, a manager who forgets to contact a potential buyer can lose much in sales.

Occasionally forgetfulness can cause heartache and pain. The lad who forgets to give his girl friend a corsage for the big dance can be in deep trouble as she suffers his apparent lack of sensitivity. Failure to remember birthdays, anniversaries and Valentine's Day can hurt another's feelings. "I completely forgot we had a date," can be devastating words to hear if you're a young man who has spent the whole week preparing for a Friday night out with the girl he thinks he loves.

Our propensity toward forgetfulness contrasts sharply with God's inability to forget. Even if a mother should forget her child — an unlikely and far-fetched idea — God can never forget his own. God remembers all his creatures — great and small — and watches over them all, especially those who were created in his own image and likeness.

Because God does not forget, he answers those in need. We may not immediately recognize or even like the answer we receive, but God, nevertheless, answers our petitions. To those who find themselves imprisoned in doubt and despair, God says, "Don't be afraid. Face your doubts and conquer your fears." To those who prefer to hide from the problems of daily living, he says, "Come to me all you who labor and are heavily burdened and I will refresh you."

God is always with us, leading us to places we dare not go on our own, satisfying our hunger with his word and quenching our thirst with streams of grace. The only thing God ever forgets is our sins, once we've confessed them. He never forsakes his people.

Meditation: When did you last forget something important? How did you feel?

Prayer: God of comfort, you cut a road through the mountains and make the highways level for your people. You call upon the heavens and the earth to rejoice and the mountains to break forth into song as you remember us, your people. Strengthen our trust. Call us out of our prisons. Remove our darkness. Let us experience your tenderness and know that you never forget us.

Make this a day of salvation through our Lord Jesus Christ, your Son, who lives and reigns with you and the Holy Spirit, one God, forever and ever. Amen.

Activity: Identify three experiences in your life when you thought that God had forgotten you. How did you feel? How did you come to know and experience the opposite, that he had remembered you?

IDOL OF FREEDOM

Scripture: The LORD said to Moses, "Go down at once to
your people, whom you brought out of the land of
Egypt. . . . They have soon turned aside from the
way I pointed out to them, making for themselves a
molten calf and worshiping it, sacrificing to it and
crying out, 'This is your God, O Israel, who brought
you out of the land of Egypt!' "   (Exodus 32:7-8)

Mass: Exodus 32:7-14; John 5:31-47

Reflection: People have a tendency to revere that which sets
them free. A group of English colonists who were fed up with
taxation without representation fought a war to gain their independence. Once free, they elected leaders who drafted a Constitution and a Bill of Rights. These documents today are
enshrined in the nation's capital where they are revered by
almost every citizen in the United States because they ensure
their freedom.
     The story of the poor boy who strikes it rich thrills
everyone. It's part of the American dream in a land of opportunity. The poor boy works hard on the family farm to save enough
money to go away to college. There he spends hours in intense
study and graduates with honors. He finds himself being sought
after by a large corporation in which he steadily advances on the
rungs of success until he becomes the president of the company.
Managing the riches he sought and acquired now takes up all his

time. He ends up enslaved to the very dollars which promised to set him free. They've become his god.

Those who struggle to keep off excess pounds can often find themselves in a similar situation. They have to be faithful to their workout at the local health club three or four times a week, watch their diet carefully by avoiding fried and fatty foods and eating plenty of low cholesterol, high protein, high fiber foods. Their life revolves around their body for which nothing is too good. The mirror becomes the shrine at which they worship.

Is it any wonder then, that the Israelites, once they were freed from Egyptian slavery, decided to produce a golden calf and worship it? The invisible God had engineered their escape; Moses had led them through the Sea of Reeds. Since he had gone up the mountain and God could not be seen, the people decided to create an image they could adore — a molten calf. Once it was fashioned from their gold, they bowed down and paid it homage. It was like the god their neighbors all adored.

Meditation: From what have you most recently been set free? In what ways did you end up enslaved to that which set you free and come to worship it?

Prayer: God of Moses, once you led your people from Egyptian slavery to desert freedom, but they created a molten calf and worshiped it as their god. Through Jesus, your servant and your Son, you have set us free from sin. Guide us with your Holy Spirit that we may never turn back and worship idols made by human hands. Enable us to praise you, the only God, who lives and reigns as Father, Son and Holy Spirit, forever and ever. Amen.

Activity: Search your life until you identify three situations from which you were set free. For each one identify the slavery, the freedom, and whether or not you created an idol out of your freedom and turned around and worshiped it.

JUST ONES

Scripture: "Let us beset the just one, because he is obnoxious to us;
he sets himself against our doings,
reproaches us for transgressions of the law
and charges us with violations of our training."

(Wisdom 2:12)

Mass: Wisdom 2:1, 12-22; John 7:1-2, 10, 25-30

Reflection: There is no person who makes other people more angry than a just one. A just person is an individual who is honest, when honesty can cost him everything. A just person is one who practices what he or she believes. For such persons attendance at the celebration of the Eucharist on Sunday has nothing to do with a law but with an inner desire to worship and thank God. Those who find time to work in the local soup kitchen, visit the sick and, in general, do good deeds, are just ones.

Many find themselves getting angry in the presence of the just because they confront them with their lack of honesty or their lack of motivation or their lack of good deeds. It is easier for everyone to keep it secret, to have seen nothing and heard nothing, than it is to tell the truth. Nothing is risked by silence; all is put on the line with honesty. It is easier to drag oneself out of bed every weekend to passively spend an hour in church than it is to prepare throughout the week for the greatest act of thanksgiving that the body of Christ can make to God. It's easier to take care of oneself first; then, if there's some time left, those who are in need and those organizations that rely on volunteers may get a piece of the pie.

The just spark jealousy in some. Others condemn them by starting rumors about them. There are those who will even set a trap in an attempt to catch the just one. Why? Because we do not like to see our own weaknesses exposed. We don't like to see our faults and failings held up before our eyes by those who exemplify what we would like or ought to be.

No human being is perfect, but there are those who are just. The problem is not with their justice, but with the failure of sinners to recognize the lack of justice in their own lives and own up to it. The just are examples of what we are all called to be. Even they often stumble and fall, but they have learned how to profit by their failures and to keep moving forward instead of wallowing in their weakness.

Meditation: Whom do you recognize as a just person? Why? How does this person affect you?

Prayer: God of the just, to those who follow your way you give knowledge and make them your children. When we are tested, give us your gifts of gentleness and patience. When we face death, give us your confidence and care. Do not let our own wickedness blind us to those who keep your word and remain just in your sight. Continue to call us to the justice for which Jesus died. We ask this through our Lord Jesus Christ, your Son, who lives and reigns with you and the Holy Spirit, one God, forever and ever. Amen.

Activity: Look back over your life and identify three just persons who, because of their sense of justice, made you angry, confronted you, or in some way were a disturbance to you. In which ways did you grow into a more just person because of their example? What did each one teach you?

SLAUGHTERED LAMB

Scripture: I, like a trusting lamb led to slaughter, had not
realized that they were hatching plots against me:
"Let us destroy the tree in its vigor; let us cut him off
from the land of the living, so that his name will be
spoken no more."   (Jeremiah 12:19)

Mass: Jeremiah 12:18-20; John 7:40-53

Reflection: It is only the very cautious individual who has never
felt like a lamb led to slaughter. Basically, most of us trust other
people. When someone tells us something, we are usually not
suspicious but accept it as the truth. When someone does us a
favor, we usually do not question the motives behind it but
simply trust the other. Likewise when others demonstrate by
word or deed their love for us, we don't look for a reason behind
it but accept that love as a free gift and trust that it is authentic.

We've all had, though, the experience of being betrayed by
another. The word spoken turns out to be nothing but another
lie intended to get even or to hurt another. The favor, so freely
done, turns out to be a subtle way of putting us in another's debt.
The love which was pledged ends up being a manipulative
technique for getting information or for pursuing some other
unworthy cause.

When we have trusted others in any way and end up being
betrayed, we feel like a lamb led to slaughter. We have put our

necks on the chopping block and lost our heads. We feel like we've been crucified. Like a trusting lamb being prepared for the holocaust, we find ourselves getting burned.

We feel like a tree which is cut down just as it reaches its peak of growth. Trust fosters growth. When we trust another, we expand our horizons, see life from a new perspective and find ourselves willing to take risks. When trust is violated, we respond by drawing boundaries much closer, retreating into the familiar and the known, pursuing courses where there are no risks. For trust to flourish there must be an environment of trust, just as for a tree to grow there must be good soil and plenty of sunshine and water.

Meditation: Whom have you trusted only to discover that you had been led to the slaughter? Whom have you led to their holocaust after they trusted you?

Prayer: God of Jeremiah, Lord of hosts, just judge, searcher of mind and heart, you rescue those who trust in you. After having been led to the cross himself, like a lamb on its way to the slaughter, Jesus, your Son, cried out to you and you answered his prayer. When our trust in others falters, make us secure in our trust of you. Continue to call us to grow that we might come to the fullness of life in the land of the living where you reign with Jesus and the Holy Spirit, one God, forever and ever. Amen.

Activity: Make a list of three people whom you have trusted only to discover that you were betrayed. What was the reason for the trust? What was the reason for the betrayal? Make a list of three people whom you have betrayed after they placed their trust in you. What was the reason for their trust? Why did you betray them?

Cycle A

COMING HOME

Scripture: Thus says the Lord GOD: O my people, I will open your graves and have you rise from them, and bring you back to the land of Israel.   (Ezekiel 37:12)

Mass: Ezekiel 37:12-14; Romans 8:8-11; John 11:1-45

Reflection: After being away, even for a short period of time, most of us are anxious to return home. "I can't wait to get back to my own house," "It sure will feel good to sleep in my own bed again," "I'm tired of living out of a suitcase; I want to get back home to my own things," are expressions we've all heard time and time again and probably even used ourselves.

Although not often associated with it, the experience of coming home is a little like rising from the dead. There is both a surface reality and a deep-down sense of truth in this thought. The surface reality is expressed when someone has died and a comforter of the grieving says, "God has called him (or her) home." This metaphorical way of speaking about the reality of death implies that God has everything under control and has bestowed eternal life on the one who has died. This person is now home with God in one of the many rooms in the Father's mansion of which Jesus spoke in the Gospel of St. John.

The deeper sense of truth is found in the daily dying and

rising that people experience. "Have you been born again?" is another way of asking, "Have you ever died and found a new life?" At first one may be taken aback by the suggestion, but on closer examination it becomes apparent that we all die and find new life many times and in many ways in the course of a lifetime. And, every time, it's a little like coming home again after having been away.

Persons, for example, can die to career decisions in college. They may have been good at many things and had the mental acumen to master almost anything they intended to do. At first the object was to make lots of money in order to live the "good life." After a fierce inner struggle, though, they abandoned this objective and embraced a life of service to others where the pay was barely adequate. They died in a sense, but their grave was opened, and they found a new life; they came back home again.

Others may find themselves struggling with a moral decision. If they tell the truth, they could lose their job — one that they had spent twenty years working toward. On the other hand, to keep quiet would mean that many people will be taken advantage of, used, and treated with no human dignity. The decision to tell the truth and to freely embrace the consequences is to experience a kind of death. Once through it, though, the individual discovers that the grave has been opened and he or she has come home.

Even children experience dying and rising. When a child freely relinquishes a cherished toy by offering it to another, that child has died to his own desires. The love, affection, and encouragement he receives for having done so are part of the new life he experiences. The child's grave has been opened and he has come home again.

People die to themselves every day. Every day they experience their graves being opened. They learn to trust death because they've know resurrection. Open graves are always the best kind.

Meditation: When did you most recently die and have a coming home experience?

Prayer: Lord God, you promised your people that you would free them from their exile and bring them home. Even though they thought that they were hopeless dry bones, you promised them open graves and new life. Breathe new life into our deaths. Give us the strength to trust your promise of open graves. Bring us home by raising us to the life which you share with your Son, our Lord Jesus Christ, who lives and reigns with you and the Holy Spirit, one God, forever and ever. Amen.

Activity: Identify three major experience of death in your life. To what did you die? What new life did you discover? How did you come home again?

Cycle B

CHOSEN HEARTS

Scripture: This is the covenant which I will make with the house of Israel . . . , says the LORD. I will place my law within them, and write it upon their hearts; I will be their God, and they shall be my people.

(Jeremiah 31:33)

Mass: Jeremiah 31:31-34; Hebrews 5:7-9; John 12:20-33

Reflection: There is a difference between a contract and a covenant. For all practical purposes a contract is a legal document which states the terms of the agreement for those signing their names on the dotted line.

For example, a publisher and an author enter into a contract; the publisher agrees to release the author's book and pay him or her a royalty based upon the sales, and the author agrees to write the book and provide any other information which is requested by the publisher.

When a person goes to the bank to procure a loan to purchase a house or car, he or she enters into a contract with the lender. The bank agrees to loan a certain amount of money at a fixed interest rate, and the individual promises to repay the funds plus the accrued interest by a certain date. Both parties sign a contract.

A trip to the grocery store is finalized by a simple contract.

Once the cart is filled with food and other items, the person wheeling the cart takes it to the check-out person, who totals up the cost of the goods. It is understood that money — either in the form of cash, check or credit card — will be exchanged for the goods in the cart. Once the transaction is completed and the groceries are placed in bags, a receipt is issued in the form of a cash register tape. This records each purchase, the date, place of purchase, sales tax charged, total amount of the purchase and the method of payment. The receipt is a record of the contract.

A covenant is not a contract. It is rather an agreement between two parties, one of whom is always more powerful than the other. One party agrees to do something for another, but the exchange will always be unequal. In other words, in a covenant one party will be the recipient and another the giver.

Such is the pact which God enters into with his people. God, the obviously more powerful party, agrees to accept us, the less powerful partner, as his own special possession. He doesn't force us into this agreement, but invites us. We remain free to withdraw from it at any time.

A covenant has, therefore, little to do with signing on the dotted line. It has a lot to do with making a commitment with one's heart. God is not interested in legal documents which bind parties whose names are inscribed with ink. God is interested in covenants which bind with his word written on human hearts. It is from the heart that love flows. It is from the heart that faithfulness emerges. From the heart we pledge fidelity to God's ways.

Through the words of the covenant, God entered into a special relationship with Abraham. After the exodus, God reaffirmed his covenant with his people through Moses. Through the blood of his Son, Jesus, God demonstrated how faithful he would be to those who accepted his freely-offered covenant. God wants to be everyone's God; we must want to be God's chosen ones.

Meditation: How have you most recently experienced the covenant that God has made with you? Explain.

Prayer: God of the covenant, you never tire or grow weary of entering into a loving relationship with your people. In the past you entered into a solemn agreement with Abraham and Moses. Through the blood of your Son, Jesus, you have bound yourself even more closely to the family of humankind. Write your law upon our hearts. Make us realize that you are our God and we are your people. We ask this through our Lord Jesus Christ, who lives and reigns with you and the Holy Spirit, one God, forever and ever. Amen.

Activity: Recall the high points of God's covenant with you during your life: baptism, confirmation, Eucharist, penance, marriage, holy orders, anointing of the sick. How did you experience God as your God and yourself as one of God's people?

Cycle C

NEW STORIES

Scripture: Thus says the LORD,
        who opens a way in the sea
        and a path in the mighty waters. . . .
    Remember not the events of the past,
        the things of long ago consider not;
    See, I am doing something new!
        Now it springs forth, do you not perceive it?
    In the desert I make a way,
        in the wasteland, rivers.

(Isaiah 43:16, 18-19)

Mass: Isaiah 43:16-21; Philippians 3:8-14; John 8:1-11

Reflection: When extended families gather together for Thanksgiving, Christmas, and Easter dinners, the older members usually tell the younger ones about "the good old days," the past. Not only are these annual stories important enough to be heard by the young, but they give both young and old alike a perspective on history and a sense of what it means to belong to a particular family.

The events of a family's past shape the family in the present. Recalling the days of the horse and buggy not only teaches something of the history of the automobile's development but also gives an appreciation for the ease of travel available in the present. The sharing of stories about long dead ancestors not only preserves their memories, but offers the present generation a sense of their family tree, of their origins, their roots. "How we used to do it" in the past gives us a perspective from which to judge how we do it now.

While many family stories concerning the past survive year after year when families gather together for special celebrations, some of them are gradually lost. The primary storytellers get old and die, and with them perish a story or two. New ones arise to take their place with new lessons to teach and new perspectives to see. In a way, this loss of some stories is necessary if new ones are ever to have a chance to be told.

God is always coming up with new stories. He is always doing new things. Such great events as the exodus, the crossing of the Sea of Reeds, and the gift of manna and quail in the desert pale in comparison to some of the things that God is doing now. Those who are alert can see his hand in everything. Those who are always looking back have some difficulty with a God who seems to relish change.

If carefully examined, the Hebrew Scriptures (Old Testament) can be seen as a record of all the new things that God is always doing. When slavery faced his people, it was God who set them free. When a sea got in the way of their escape, it was God who parted the waters and made a path through the reeds. When there was no food or water in the desert, it was he who provided manna and quail from the skies and water from the rock.

The New Testament is a record of the new things that God did and does in Jesus. When people were in bondage to Satan and to sin, it was God who offered them freedom and forgiveness through Jesus. When access to God was blocked by the professional religious, he cut a new path through the teaching and example of Jesus. When there was no food and drink for those who hungered and thirsted for justice, it was God who, through Jesus, provided them with the body and blood of his Son.

God is still doing new things. As long as we remain open to the possibility and do not get stuck in the past, we will be able to discern these modern day wonders. The birth of a healthy child to expectant parents, the rosy orange of a silent winter sunrise, the peaceful death of an aged loved one, reveal his loving and creative hand.

While it is important to remember the past, it is more important to look forward to the future. The past cannot be relived, only remembered. The future holds the potential for new life.

Meditation: When did you most recently experience God doing something new?

Prayer: God of newness, once you freed your people from slavery, opened a path in the mighty waters of the sea, provided manna from heaven, and caused water to gush forth from a rock. Through Jesus, your Son, you set us free from our sins, washed us clean in the death-dealing waters of baptism, and offered us his body and blood for nourishment and strength. Guide us now with your Holy Spirit. Open our eyes to see the wonders that you set before us every day. Help us to recognize your presence in all that you create. We ask this through our Lord Jesus Christ, who lives and reigns with you and the Holy Spirit, one God, forever and ever. Amen.

Activity: What three major events of your past do you consider to be times when God did something new in your life? In what three events of the future do you hope to find God doing something new in your life?

IDENTIFICATION

Scripture: When Elisha reached the house, he found the boy
lying dead. He went in, closed the door . . . , and
prayed to the LORD. Then he lay upon the child on
the bed, placing his mouth upon the child's mouth,
his eyes upon the eyes, and his hands upon the
hands. As Elisha stretched himself over the child,
the body became warm.   (2 Kings 4:32-34)

Mass: 2 Kings 4:18-21, 32-37; John 11:1-45

Reflection: In order to understand someone else we must
identify with that person as fully as possible. Today, this is
occasionally accomplished in one or another of the many different support groups that exist. If you want to understand what it
means to stop smoking, all you have to do is join a support group
which is composed of others who are trying to quit or have
already stopped themselves. There is an empathy in the group.
The members understand one another.

Someone interested in dieting, but who has repeatedly
tried and given up, might try to join a weight watchers group. All
the members share the same problems associated with dieting;
each one understands the weakness of the others.

People who have recently experienced the death of a rela-
tive or close friend similarly often find comfort in a grieving

group where they share with others the grieving process. Shared compassion leads to healing. One person fosters and supports another's healing by empathizing with that person.

This "being with" or "feeling with" or "union with" is raised to a sublime level as a result of the Incarnation. When the eternal Word of God became a man and lived among us, he took on our human nature with all its ramifications. God became vulnerable, subject to all that we experience. Henceforth no one could ever say that God did not understand. The compassion of Jesus brought healing to the human race. Because he is able to sympathize with our human weakness, he is able to help us overcome it. Because he is God he is able to raise us up to new life.

The prophet Elisha was a man who entered deeply into the sufferings of others. He did this in the case of the Shunammite's dead son. He identified himself with the little boy by stretching himself upon him, placing his mouth, eyes, and hands upon those of the child. In a prayer filled with profound compassion, he pleaded with God for the life of the boy. His spirit became one with that of God and of the little boy. And because of this identification, the child opened his eyes. God gave him back his life.

Those who are willing to identify with others continue to accomplish in an analogous way what Elisha did for the Shunammite's child. They dispel pain, offer a sense of solidarity, console, and encourage. They restore hope, and hence life, to others.

We express our compassion when we share our life experiences with one another through words, looks and tender touches. Such identification with what the other is going through can bring about healing and new resolve. It can restore one to life again.

Meditation: When did you most recently find yourself

identifying with another? What was the occasion? How did your understanding help to heal the other?

Prayer: God of life and death, when the son of the Shunammite woman slept in death, you sent your prophet Elisha to bring him back to life again. In the fullness of time you sent your only Son, Jesus, in human flesh to identify with and bring new life to the human race. When we suffer, send another to heal us. Through him or her stretch out your hand and raise us up. May we always praise you for the life we now share and for the eternal life to come where you live and reign with Jesus and the Holy Spirit, one God, forever and ever. Amen.

Activity: Recall three instances in your life when you were suffering and another person was able to identify with you and enter into your pain. Write these down and indicate for each who your healer was and how he or she healed you. How was your life changed?

TRUTH

Scripture: As [Susanna] was being led to execution, God stir-
red up the holy spirit of a young boy named Daniel,
and he cried aloud: "I will have no part in the death
of this woman. Are you such fools, O Israelites! To
condemn a woman of Israel without examination
and without clear evidence? Return to court, for [the
two elders] have testified falsely against her."
                                            (Daniel 13:45-46, 48-49)

Mass: Daniel 13:1-9, 15-17, 19-30, 33-62;
            (Years A and B) John 8:1-11 or (Year C) John 8:12-20

Reflection: As soon as most of us do something that is wrong,
we try to hide or cover up our error almost instinctively. We do it
at times to protect our reputation, job or sense of self-esteem.
When we find ourselves in the middle of a mistake, we feel that
we must preserve what others have thought of us, our work or
our authority.

Sometimes we do this at the expense of another. In our
technological age, we try to blame the computer, but the
operator is usually found to be at fault. If the problem is really
serious, we may choose to resign rather than be fired. For most
of us, it's very important to save face.

Human weakness is the culprit. What we often fail to realize
is that there are no perfect people. By the very fact of being
human, we are prone to make mistakes. The attempt to cover up
our misdeeds is reminiscent of Adam's fault and also bespeaks our
fallen human state. That doesn't, however, exonerate us.

The story of Susanna and the two elders of Israel is a good example of how one sin leads to another. Lust led the two elders to desire to lie with Susanna. When she refused, they decided to get even with her. After all, as a woman her testimony would almost certainly be rejected in the face of the deposition of the two elders.

These two crafty elders forgot one thing, however — that God is on the side of truth. His wisdom cannot be hidden or concealed by sin. He raises up those who recognize the truth and are willing to proclaim it to others, even when the others would rather not hear it. The prophets are the best examples of God's truth-speakers.

Through Daniel the sins of the two elders of Israel are revealed. Susanna is found innocent and is spared. Human judges had erred because they held no monopoly on the truth. Truth, though, will triumph over sin — sooner or later. Truth is God's own way.

Meditation: In what situation did you find yourself most recently attempting to figure out a way to avoid telling the truth? Did truth finally come out?

Prayer: God of Susanna and Daniel, you know what is hidden and are aware of all that is, even before these come to pass. You save those who place their trust in you. Fill us with your Holy Spirit of truth that we might always have the courage to face what is true and to accept what is right. We ask this through your Son, Jesus, who is our Way, our Truth, and our Life, and who lives with you and the Holy Spirit, one God, forever and ever. Amen.

Activity: Try to think of three incidents in which truth won out over falsehood and the innocent were set free. How was God's hand made manifest in their release? Has anything similar ever happened to you?

SNAKES

Scripture: The LORD said to Moses, "Make a saraph and
mount it on a pole, and if anyone who has been
bitten looks at it, he [or she] will recover." Moses
accordingly made a bronze serpent and mounted it
on a pole, and whenever anyone who had been
bitten by a serpent looked at the bronze serpent, he
[or she] recovered.   (Numbers 21:8-9)

Mass: Numbers 21:4-9; John 8:21-30

Reflection: All you have to do is mention the word "snake" and
people break out in goose flesh. In pet shops, the snake pit is the
least visited of all the areas; those who do dare to walk there view
the various intertwined serpents warily through protective glass.
The "Do Not Tap On The Glass" sign is carefully observed by
most patrons. If a snake is encountered in one's yard or garden,
both serpent and human being take off in opposite directions.
For whatever reason, most people are not attracted to snakes.
    Such dislike for the slithering serpent is not in keeping with
the religious traditions of many people of the past. For some of
these primitive cultures, the snake was a sign of wisdom and
healing. Because the snake was usually found near water, and
water was regarded as the seat of primordial wisdom, the snake
was considered a very wise creature. The snake was also looked

upon as a sign of healing, immortality, and rejuvenation because it sheds its skin annually and emerges with regained youth. In fact, a snake with its tail in its mouth, forming a circle, was often used to symbolize eternity.

Today, in doctors' offices and on the walls of medical buildings one can see a staff with one or two serpents coiled about it. The serpent-entwined staff, called a caduceus, signifies both the body's currents and the windings of the soul's evolutionary path. The healer takes both body and soul into consideration.

The evil quality often associated with the snake is due to the venom found in the snake's fangs and its ability to strike quickly, silently, and mortally.

Using the reference to Moses' construction of the healing bronze serpent in the desert, the author of John's Gospel sees Jesus as the one who heals the human race. In his dialogue with Nicodemus, Jesus says, "Just as Moses lifted up the serpent in the desert, so must the Son of Man be lifted us, so that everyone who believes in him may have eternal life" (John 3:14-15).

For John, "lifting up" refers to the cross, the sign of glorification. Jesus, exalted on the cross and through his resurrection, represents healing and eternal life for everyone. Stained glass windows and other forms of Christian art have often portrayed the union of the bronze serpent and the crucifixion of Jesus with a serpent wound around a cross. Just as the serpent in the desert brought healing for the Israelites, so does the cross bring healing to all.

Meditation: How do you react to snakes? Why do you react in this way?

Prayer: God of Moses and Jesus, when your people acknowledged their sin of complaining in the desert, you instructed

Moses, your prophet, to make a bronze serpent and mount it on a pole, so that whoever had been bitten by a serpent and looked at it would be healed. When the human race had strayed far from you, you sent your only Son, Jesus, to be lifted up in glory on the cross so that whoever looked at him and believed might have their sins forgiven and receive the gift of eternal life. Continue to pour out on us the healing gift of your Holy Spirit that we might recognize our sins, repent, and come to share the life of the kingdom, where you live and reign with Jesus and the Holy Spirit, one God, forever and ever. Amen.

Activity: Make a list of three places which you associate with healing for yourself or for someone you know. What type of healing took place? Where can you find the caduceus, the serpent-entwined staff, in your area? What type of healing occurs in these places?

TRUST AND RISK

Scripture: Nebuchadnezzar exclaimed, "Blessed be the God of Shadrach, Meshach, and Abednego, who sent his angel to deliver the servants that trusted in him; they disobeyed the royal command and yielded their bodies rather than serve or worship any god except their own God."   (Daniel 3:95)

Mass: Daniel 3:14-20, 91-92, 95; John 8:31-42

Reflection: People trust one another all the time, but seldom do they give any thought to the risk involved. Someone tells you that her mother or father has died and you rely on the truth of this information without giving it another thought. Employers place their confidence in their employees' ability to get the job done, without worrying about them walking away from the uncompleted project. Family members rely on each other to do certain daily chores: shopping, laundry, dishes, paying the bills, taking out the garbage, etc. Each one trusts the other to do his or her share.

Whether we are aware of it or not, every act of trust carries with it a certain amount of risk, the risk that the trust placed in another will be betrayed. Once trust is lost, it is hard to regain.

Consider the case of a best friend to whom you entrust some highly confidential information. When a third party comments on this privileged information, you know immediately that your friend has betrayed your trust and you'll be very careful about what you say in that person's presence in the future.

An employer who depends upon an employee to accomplish certain tasks will seek another if the first one does not do an adequate job. Family members who prove themselves to be unreliable are made to feel the resentment the others feel in a wide variety of ways. Losing privileges and denying responsibility are just two of them. May it never be said, referring to us, "If you want something done right around here, you'd better plan to do it yourself."

The trust we place in one another and the corresponding risk we take condition the trust we are apt to place in God. If our experiences in trusting others, who can be seen, have been positive, we will find it easier to trust in an invisible God, who cannot be seen.

This is what faith is all about. Faith is trust in One who cannot be seen. It is a radical conviction that God is reliable and dependable and will not abandon us. Faith is confidence that God will continue to be with us, even in the most trying circumstances of our lives. There is no proof available for this type of faith. There are, however, examples from the past which confirm God's reliability.

Shadrach, Meshach and Abednego are examples which demonstrate God's fidelity to those who place their faith in him. Rather than worship the statue which Nebuchadnezzar had commissioned, these three young men placed their trust in God. They were willing to be thrown into a fiery furnace and put to death rather than abandon their faith in God. And their trust in him was not ill founded, for miraculously they were rescued by him.

The example of their tenacious trust in God, even at the risk of losing their lives, led Nebuchadnezzar to believe. The trust that we demonstrate in the face of even lesser risks can lead others to faith as well.

Meditation: When has another person's example of faith in the face of risk strengthened your own trust in God? When has your example strengthened another's faith?

Prayer: God of Shadrach, Meshach, and Abednego, you sent your angel to deliver your servants who trusted in you. They disobeyed human authorities in order to demonstrate their trust in you. When we face the risks of living, send your Holy Spirit to fill us with the fire of unwavering faith. May the example of those who place their confidence in you be our strength. May our example be the food that supports others. Blessed are you, and praiseworthy, Father, Son, and Holy Spirit. Glorious forever is your holy name. You live and reign, one God, forever and ever. Amen.

Activity: Identify three people who have been examples of trust in God in the face of risk for you. How did each of them support your trust in God?

NAME

Scripture: When Abram prostrated himself, God continued to
speak to him: "My covenant with you is this: you are
to become the father of a host of nations. No longer
shall you be called Abram; your name shall be
Abraham, for I am making you the father of a host
of nations."
                                                (Genesis 17:3-5)

Mass: Genesis 17:3-9; John 8:51-59

Reflection: Everything and everyone has a name. We name
rivers, streams and waterfalls; trails, roads, and highways; trains,
cars, and airplanes; newspapers, magazines, and books; dogs,
cats and goldfish. We name one another.

It's important that everything and everyone have a name.
We're able to make reference to persons and things by calling
them by name. We could hardly carry on a conversation or teach
another anything if there were no such things as names.

Inanimate objects cannot think about the names they have.
We, however, can. Though we had no choice in the names we
were given, we learn to live with them. If we are unhappy with
them, we can change them later on in life. Our name is so
important that it is written on everything associated with us
from our birth certificate up to and including our death
certificate.

In between we write our names on everything from birthday cards to homework assignments, credit cards to letters, contracts to permits, licenses to checks. In fact, a day seldom passes when we don't sign our name on something.

In ancient days, a person's name told everyone something about the person. A person's name described the individual in some way. Abram was called Abram because his name means "a father is exalted." Indeed, the father of Israel was an exalted man. However, after entering into a covenant with God, Abram's name was changed to Abraham to indicate the change which had taken place in him. His new name means "father of a host of nations." God promised Abram that he would multiply him; that is, that he would have many descendants and that his posterity would become a nation dear to God. In order to indicate this new relationship with God, Abram became Abraham, the great grandfather of a host of nations.

Before requesting baptism for their children, parents give their offspring names. Adults, before their baptism, choose a name for themselves. By these names they will be known in the community. In some sense, these names also describe the individuals who are entering into the covenant-making waters of new life. As they die to their old way of living, they rise to a new way of life; they enter into a covenant with God who calls each of them by name.

Meditation: Does your name describe you and your relationship with God? In what ways?

Prayer: God of Abraham, by name you called your servant and entered into a covenant with him. You made him the father of many nations, and you never abandoned him. Through the blood of Jesus, your Son, you entered into a covenant with us. You did not abandon him on the cross, but rather made him the source of the new life of your Church. Keep us faithful to our baptismal calling. Through the guidance of your Holy Spirit enable us to be true to the Christian name we bear. We ask this through our Lord Jesus Christ, who lives and reigns with you and the Holy Spirit, one God, forever and ever. Amen.

Activity: Go to a library or other resource center and find out the etymology (history of the origin) of your name. What does your name mean? In what ways does the name "Christian" describe you?

WHISPERINGS

Scripture: Yes, I hear the whisperings of many:
          "Terror on every side!
          Denounce! let us denounce him!"
        All those who were my friends
          are on the watch for any misstep of mine.
        "Perhaps he will be trapped; then we can prevail,
          and take our vengeance on him."

(Jeremiah 20:10)

Mass: Jeremiah 20:10-13; John 10:31-42

Reflection: Most of us at one time or another have been guilty of talking about others behind their backs. The reasons are many. We may not want to embarrass them by confronting them with something unbecoming in their demeanor or dress. So instead of telling them about it so that they could do something to remedy the situation, we whisper it to others who spread it even further.

At times we repeat rumors in a whisper because we're not sure of the degree of truth behind them. "She's getting a divorce." "I hear he was called into the boss's office." "John's dad grounded him for a month." Instead of asking the subject involved about the truth behind the rumor, we keep the gossip mill grinding. And, of course, the story grows the more it spreads.

Passing on secret information can be a way of getting even

with someone. Two friends have a falling out. One tells his or her side of the story and purposely leaves out half the truth. The one who hears the story is naturally inclined to take the side of the story-teller and thinks critically of the other.

Honest people can be the object of lunchroom whisperings at times. Because they always tell the truth — even when it is inopportune or not advantageous — they are frequently disliked. Others wait for an occasion to entrap them in a momentary lapse in character. That way, they don't look so bad themselves. All of us have chinks in our armor which can be pierced.

Whispers, rumors, talking behind another person's back can lead those talked about to the brink of despair. Ultimately, of course, those who engage in such things are the losers, though for awhile it may seem that they have triumphed. Truth generally has a way of coming out and the innocent are vindicated. God does not abandon his own; he rescues them. He is always on the side of truth.

Meditation: Most recently, when have you been the object of the whisperings of others? When have you most recently whispered about people to others?

Prayer: God of Jeremiah, when your prophet was in despair, you did not abandon him, but filled him with the courage of prophecy. As you test the just and probe minds and hearts, may you find us free from sin. Fill us with your Spirit of love for all. Rescue us from those who whisper against us and from those who denounce us. Then we shall sing to you and praise you, Father, Son, and Holy Spirit, one God, living and reigning forever and ever. Amen.

Activity: Make a list of three times in the past that, by the grace of God, the truth set you free, when others were spreading rumors about you or talking about you behind your back. Make a list of three times in the past that you spread rumors or talked about another, then discovered that you were wrong. How did you restore the dignity and integrity of the other person's reputation? What have you learned from these experiences?

UNION AT HOME

Scripture: I will take the Israelites from among the nations to which they have come, and gather them from all sides to bring them back to their land. I will make them one nation upon the land, in the mountains of Israel, and there shall be one prince for them all. Never again shall they be two nations, and never again shall they be divided into two kingdoms.

(Ezekiel 37:21-22)

Mass: Ezekiel 37:21-28; John 11:45-57

Reflection: Most of us like to travel in order to see new places and to meet new people. At the same time, we like the feeling of coming home, no matter how short a time we've been away. Home is where the heart is. Home is where we feel safe. We find ideal comfort in our home because it conforms to and is made in the image of those of us who live there. There is, therefore, always something special about coming home.

There are many in the world who have left their homes never to return again. Often these persons were forced out of their homes by governments. Sometimes they were compelled to flee their homelands in order to save their lives. Others leave their homes and emigrate to a new country buoyed up by the hope and the promise of opportunity.

Wherever they find themselves, these persons — who

cannot return home for whatever reasons — must begin the task of establishing a new home, a new place fit for them in which they can find shelter, rest, and comfort.

After the Israelites had been taken from their home in Jerusalem as prisoners of war to Babylon, a land of exile, in 587 B.C., God promised them that he would bring them back to their own land. God's people had become like a broken stick — divided. Through the prophecy of Ezekiel, however, God foretold the day when the two pieces of the stick would be reunited and the people would become one nation under one messianic king. Politically, this never happened.

Christians, however, believe that Jesus not only reunited Israel, but that he also made it possible for all people to form one kingdom. He did not fulfill the earthly, political expectations of what the Messiah was supposed to be. He was not a king who waged war and conquered other peoples. Rather he sought the union of all people through love. By teaching people how to live in harmony with each other, Jesus, the Son of God, established a kingdom of justice and peace which he called the kingdom of God.

Today, more than ever, many continue to seek for political solutions to kingdom problems. Instead of attempting to view the bigger picture, the focus is on the imbalance of power, problems with trade, making more money in the stock market. All this pales into insignificance in the light of the eternal kingdom of God. If we were to seek union with one another through Christian love, the establishment of that kingdom would more quickly take place. Our true home has been purchased for us by the suffering, death, resurrection, and ascension of Jesus and the title handed over to us in the gift of the Holy Spirit. Unfortunately, many have not found their way home yet.

Meditation: When was the last time that you were away from home and experienced an overwhelming desire to return? What makes your home so special? What type of family unity exists in your home?

Prayer: God of Ezekiel, when your people were exiled from their own land and taken as prisoners of war to Babylon, you did not abandon them. Through your prophet you promised them that you would reunite them and bring them home. Through the suffering, death, resurrection, ascension, and gift of the Spirit of Jesus you have made it possible for all to come home to your kingdom. When we tend to divide, fill us with the Spirit of unity. What we separate, we ask you to make one through your Son, our Lord Jesus Christ, who lives and reigns with you and the Holy Spirit, one God, forever and ever. Amen.

Activity: Make a list of three times when you recognized the unity between people and did not focus on their divisions. How were these experiences glimpses of the kingdom of God?

Cycles A, B and C

CALLED

Scripture: The Lord GOD has given me
                 a well-trained tongue,
               That I might know how to speak to the weary
                 a word that will rouse them.
               Morning after morning
                 he opens my ear that I may hear;
               And I have not rebelled,
                 have not turned back.

(Isaiah 50:4-5)

Mass: Procession with Palms:
                 Year A - Matthew 21:1-11
                 Year B - Mark 11:1-10 or John 12:12-16
                 Year C - Luke 19:28-40
               Liturgy of the Word: Isaiah 50:4-7; Philippians 2:6-11
                 Year A - Matthew 26:14 - 27:66
                 Year B - Mark 14:1 - 15:47
                 Year C - Luke 22:14 - 23:56

Reflection: All of us receive calls at one time or another — a
wake-up call in the morning, a shout across the field to get our
attention, the ringing of a telephone.
       As we call one another, so God calls us. And just as we are

free to respond or not to others' calls, so we are free to answer or not the call of God. The Lord calls us to follow him in a specific way of life which we speak of as our vocation, our calling, but he always leaves us free to accept or reject his offer. God calls some to be teachers, lawyers, doctors, secretaries, electrical line persons, parents, writers, priests, brothers, sisters. Many times we are called to fulfill more than one role. At any rate, the list is endless. What every calling or vocation in life has in common is this: the grace to respond to the call as God desires. Preachers are given well-trained tongues in order to exhort people and move their hearts to conversion. Teachers are given the ability to convey knowledge to their students and to spark in them a desire to learn. Parents are given the grace to love, support, and care for their children physically, emotionally, and spiritually.

The problem we encounter in our society today, though, is that the lure of money, the desire for power or prestige often drowns out God's call. When that happens, his will is not accomplished and our lives remain in some significant way unfulfilled.

It's not always easy to hear God's call and to do his will. It takes time to discern — in silence and through prayer — what precisely it is that God is calling us to do. Jesus, God's own Son, stands as our model of one who spent much time in silence, listening for the will of the Father in his prayer. And then he became all that the Father desired: "This is my beloved Son in whom I am well pleased." Jesus did not rebel, even in the face of death. He did not turn back, even when handed the cross. We are called to that kind of faithfulness in following our own vocations.

Meditation: To what vocation or way of life has God called you? In what ways did you discern this calling? What problems have you experienced in accepting it?

Prayer: Lord God, you are the help of all who call on you. To every one of us you issue an invitation to follow you in a specific way of life. Through the working of your Holy Spirit, help us to know what you ask of us and give us the grace to do it. Train our tongues to speak your word as you open our ears to hear your will. When we falter, remind us of your servant Jesus, who did not rebel nor turn back from the cross. We ask this through our Lord Jesus Christ, your Son, who lives and reigns with you and the Holy Spirit, one God, forever and ever. Amen.

Activity: Trace the steps of your life's vocation. In other words, make a list of the experiences of your past which have confirmed for you the vocation to which God has called you. How can these past experiences help guide you in making future choices?

JUSTICE

Scripture: I, the LORD, have called you for the victory
                     of justice,
                 I have grasped you by the hand;
                 I formed you, and set you
                     as a covenant of the people,
                     a light for the nations,
                 To open the eyes of the blind,
                     to bring out prisoners from confinement,
                     and from the dungeon, those who live in darkness.
                                                     (Isaiah 42:6-7)

Mass: Isaiah 42:1-7; John 12:1-11

Reflection: The word "justice" is almost always used in-
terchangeably with the word "jurisprudence" and made to refer
to a system of legal courts in which one's case is heard and a
decision is reached either by a judge or a jury. While a legal
system might be considered synonymous with justice, it doesn't
get to the core of what biblical justice is all about.
      Biblical justice is of the heart. It isn't concerned with what is
or is not legal — what can or cannot be done within the law.
Rather it asks what should or should not be done from a moral
perspective. When people practice biblical justice, they take into
account the equal and common human dignity of others and are
directed by this consideration.

For example, it might be legal to hire an employee for the federal minimum wage. However, if that employee has a family or if the cost of living makes a dramatic rise, is it still just to continue to pay that employee the same salary as you might a young kid in high school? How does a person's salary support his or her human dignity? Is biblical justice rendered by adhering to strict legal jurisprudence?

What about those employees who cheat their employer by taking longer breaks than stipulated or by coming late and leaving early? Are they practicing biblical justice? Legally, a few minutes here and a few minutes there are not worth worrying about. Biblically, the employee is obliged to give an employer a fair day's work for a fair day's wage.

Honesty, in terms of telling the truth, is also part of biblical justice. Our sense of biblical justice is put to the test when we're called upon to speak the truth when doing so may prove costly to us. Can we remain just and still lie? Can we hide the truth about another, when revealing the truth would entail our getting deeply involved in something we'd prefer to stay out of, if many will be hurt by our concealing it?

Every day we're faced with matters of biblical justice. In many cases, we're legally protected. However, if we are authentic followers of Jesus, we will always opt for what supports the equal and common human dignity of all. We are to be a light for others. By standing firm and giving a good example, we may open the eyes of those who are blinded by the legality of a matter. We may be able to lead forth from their personal prisons those who have confined their moral activity to the level of mere jurisprudence. Biblical justice is a victory that is won in the heart.

Meditation: When have you recently found yourself caught between legality and biblical justice? What was the issue? What decision did you reach? Was your decision biblically as well as legally just?

Prayer: God of justice, you chose Jesus, your servant and your Son, for the victory of justice. By pouring out your Spirit upon him you enabled him to teach all peoples. You made of his blood a covenant. Fill us with the same Spirit that we might be strengthened in our work for justice. Help us to recognize the equal and common human dignity of every person. Grasp each of us by hand and lead us to the kingdom where you live and reign with Jesus and the Holy Spirit, one God, forever and ever. Amen.

Activity: Name three situations in which you have found yourself having to make a choice between merely observing the law and the cost of observing justice. In each situation what decision did you make? Why? What was the price to be paid for biblical justice? What did you learn from each of these experiences?

FROM ETERNITY

Scripture: The LORD called me from birth,
        from my mother's womb he gave me my name.
    He made of me a sharp-edged sword
        and concealed me in the shadow of his arm.
    He made me a polished arrow,
        in his quiver he hid me.
    You are my servant, he said to me,
        Israel, through whom I show my glory.

                                    (Isaiah 49:1-3)

Mass: Isaiah 49:1-6; John 13:21-33, 36-38

Reflection: It's an awesome thought to consider that you were called by God from before the time you were even conceived in your mother's womb, and that he even gave you a special name. Before you had ears to hear the call or a tongue to pronounce your acceptance, God called you and gave you a name.

The Lord calls each of us before we even exist to be his own. Each one of us has been allotted a special position or office, to be one of his people. Our God is madly in love with us; he will do all in his power to get us to respond to his love and to answer his call.

If we choose to answer his call, then God makes us like a two-edged sword and enables us to cut through to the heart of things to determine what is of God and what is not. Once we answer his call, we begin to see things through a new lens. All of creation takes on increased value and becomes precious in our sight. Each human being is seen as endowed with special dignity and worth. Every word is understood as laden with a message from God. Our perspective changes and we learn to see things from God's point of view and to discern his holy will.

We find protection in God when we respond to his call. God is like a mother who welcomes her children who come running up to her, wrapping themselves in the folds of her dress and clinging to her legs for protection. Hidden in their mother's shadow, they find security. God shields us in the shadow of his arm.

When we've accepted God's call to holiness and integrity, we may discover that we are not unlike polished arrows, darting here and there through life with an ability to zero in on what is just and to target that which is not. With a luster that reflects the Son, we gain respect from others as persons who represent what is right and true.

We don't try to force others into our way of life but offer them an opportunity to consider it through our example. We become like arrows hidden in God's quiver, ready to be used by him when he is ready to shoot a good example across the path of others.

Those who hear God's call and attempt to do God's will are vehicles for the revelation of his glory. What they manifest is not their own goodness or power, but God's grace, his willingness to use human beings to do more than they ever dreamed possible. All this because they responded to his call which was voiced before they ever came to be.

Meditation: When did you most recently hear God's call? To what was he summoning you? How did you respond? What were the results?

Prayer: Lord God, from before we were conceived in our
mother's womb, you called us to be your servants by hearing
your word and doing your will. Through Jesus, your servant and
your Son, you have revealed your name and your glory. Open
our hearts to hear the words you speak. Do not permit us to toil
in vain or to uselessly spend our strength. Through your Holy
Spirit, give us direction and protection; make of us a sharp-edged
sword hidden in the shadow of your arm; form us into polished
arrows, hidden in the quiver of your love. One day may we come
to share in the glory which is yours, Father, Son, and Holy Spirit,
one God, forever and ever. Amen.

Activity: Identify three past experiences when you heard
God's call. In which ways did God make you like a sharp-edged
sword or a polished arrow? How did God reveal his glory
through you?

HELP

Scripture: He is near who upholds my right;
        if anyone wishes to oppose me,
        let us appear together.
     Who disputes my right?
     Let him confront me.
     See, the Lord GOD is my help;
        who will prove me wrong?

(Isaiah 50:8-9)

Mass: Isaiah 50:4-9; Matthew 26:14-25

Reflection: If you're preparing a vegetable garden for planting and notice that the time is growing short, you might ask someone else to help you. After writing a story for the local newspaper or an article for a magazine, you might ask another writer for an opinion regarding the piece. A father might ask his son to help him wash the car, a mother might ask for help with the garbage or the dishes or the housecleaning.

In all these cases, a task needs to be done and help is required in doing it. When we need help, we don't hesitate to ask others to come to our rescue. As human beings we rely on one another to help us with our work.

We have to be careful, though, that we don't take advantage of others and try to play God. It's one thing to value our independence and to like to be in control at all times; it's quite another to gain that independence and exercise that control at the expense of others.

When we assume a position of superiority with respect to another, we are playing God and assuming his rightful role. All of us are subject to him and must learn from him how we are to treat one another. He came, not to be served, but to serve and to give his life as a ransom for the many. Each of us is called, therefore, to a life of service not unlike his own. Each of us receives the help we need from God in order that we might make the contribution that he expects from us for the good of all.

In God's eyes we are all equal. No one is greater than another in his estimation. Any authority that one may have comes from him. He helps all of us alike and calls us to be his own co-workers. We share equally in the need to help one another and to ask each other for assistance.

Meditation: When have you most recently found yourself in the position of being an authentic co-worker of another? When were you recently treated as slave labor? Which did you prefer and why?

Prayer: Lord God, you are the help of all. You bring us to birth and make us your co-workers. When we fall into the sin of self-reliance, awaken us to the light of your grace that sustains us. When we play God, remind us of our common human state. Give us the help of your Holy Spirit, who lives and reigns with you, Father, and your Son, our Lord Jesus Christ, one God, forever and ever. Amen.

Activity: Identify three times when you were asked to help others. What were you asked to do? Were you treated as a co-worker or a slave? Identify three occasions when you asked others to help you. What did you ask them to do? How did you treat them? Explain.

Chrism Mass

ANOINTED CHOICE

Scripture: The spirit of the Lord GOD is upon me,
            because the LORD has anointed me;
        He has sent me to bring glad tidings to the lowly,
            to heal the brokenhearted,
        To proclaim liberty to the captives
            and release to the prisoners,
        To announce a year of favor from the LORD
            and a day of vindication by our God,
            to comfort all who mourn.

(Isaiah 61:1-2)

Mass: Isaiah 61:1-3, 6, 8-9; Revelation 1:5-8; Luke 4:16-21

Reflection: All of us have had the experience of being chosen.
We may have been chosen to take a part in a kindergarten play,
or to be on a grade school basketball or football team. As an
adult, perhaps we were chosen to be a marriage partner, or for a
new position in the company, or for a raise.

Whenever we're chosen, we take on new responsibilities. If
we're chosen to be in the kindergarten play, we have to learn our
lines. If we're selected for the basketball team, we accept responsibility for training, attending practices, and playing to win.
The same is true in forming a family, or working in a business.

When God chooses us, he gives us responsibilities. But he also gives us a share of his Spirit. Just as an aching muscle is anointed with a soothing salve or oil, so God anoints his chosen people with his Spirit. He shares with them something of himself.

Those chosen by God are responsible for sharing the good news with others. The lowly or depressed need words which will pick them up. Sometimes it's hard to offer good news in a world that seems to thrive on bad. But those chosen by the Lord understand their mission to say a word that will heal the brokenhearted or comfort those in sorrow.

They likewise accept responsibility for proclaiming liberty to captives. There are those who take themselves hostage. They fear sharing new ideas, meeting new people, facing their own problems. Through the loving presence and sympathetic ear of those chosen by God, they can be helped to embrace the freedom that God is offering them, and to plan for the day of their release.

Those upon whom God has poured his Spirit see the world differently. Instead of being a fearful place to live, the world for them is a theophany, a manifestation of God. Instead of thinking of God as an old man who is waiting for them to make a mistake, they picture him as a loving Father who rocks his children to sleep on his lap. Instead of counting how many things can go wrong in a day, they rather count their blessings. And 365 days of favor from the Lord add up to a year of grace.

Every day presents a new opportunity to experience God's salvation. To be saved by God is to be chosen, anointed, blessed with God's Holy Spirit. Every moment of every day, every problem or joy, every word of good or fearful news, every taste of freedom or awareness of captivity is an opportunity to accept one's responsibilities as an anointed child of God.

Meditation: When did you most recently experience God's Spirit at work in your life? What was the responsibility that was entrusted to you? How did you accept it?

Prayer: Lord God, you send your Spirit upon your chosen people and you anoint them with a mission. Continue to breathe into us the strength to accept our responsibilities. Send us with good news to the lowly and brokenhearted. Give us a word for the captive and the prisoner that will set them free. Make of our lives a proclamation of the great favors that you grant to those who trust in you. We ask this, Father, through our Lord Jesus Christ, your Son, who lives and reigns with you and the Holy Spirit, one God, forever and ever. Amen.

Activity: Name an experience that you had of bringing good news to someone, of assisting in another person's freedom, and of announcing the favors of God. For each of these identify how the Spirit of the Lord was upon you. How did God anoint you?

Mass of the Lord's Supper

SHEDDING BLOOD

Scripture: "Tell the whole community of Israel: On the tenth of this month every one of your families must procure for itself a lamb, one apiece for each household. You shall keep it until the fourteenth day of this month, and then, with the whole assembly of Israel present, it shall be slaughtered during the evening twilight. They shall take some of its blood and apply it to the two doorposts and the lintel of every house in which they partake of the lamb. It is the Passover of the LORD. For on this same night I will go through Egypt, striking down every first-born of the land. . . . But the blood will mark the houses where you are. Seeing the blood, I will pass over you."
(Exodus 12:3, 6-7, 11-13)

Mass: Exodus 12:1-8, 11-14; 1 Corinthians 11:23-26; John 13:1-15

Reflection: In the course of our lives, we all discover that we've passed over from one way of life to another. The love-struck high school boy-girl relationship becomes one of responsible adult love. In marriage two individuals join themselves in wedlock and both pass over from a life alone to a life that's shared.

When faced with cancer and its treatment, people pass over from one view of life as eternal to another in which life is perceived in its finite quality. In making moral decisions people pass from one perception of reality to another. When struggling with the decision to place parents in a nursing home, adult children pass over from what they would prefer to what is best for their parents.

Every time there is a passover there is a shedding of blood. It may not be the kind of blood that courses through our veins, but it is real nonetheless. The possessive love of adolescence has to be shed if the adolescent is to be able to enter into a freeing adult relationship. Emotional blood is poured out as the teenager searches for a new way of loving another. Ask a married couple how much blood each has shed to mold their life together. A lot of individual wants and needs had to be sacrificed in order to preserve the marriage.

Facing death causes much emotional blood to be shed. The agony that a person goes through while confronting the inevitable is often devastating not only to him or her but to those around them. Moral decisions can be agonizing, and cause one to shed some more emotional blood. The prospect of not being able to care for one's family as one would like, or of having to consign a member to a nursing home can cause a heart to bleed.

But in each of these passovers there is also a sign of life. Sometimes it is hard to see, but it is there. In fact, paradoxically, life is always abundantly present when death is being confronted. The mystery lies in the fact that when we are willing to freely enter into death, instead of trying to preserve an old life, we discover a new life that is abundant and free.

Teenagers who give up an adolescent crush often feel like they are dying inside. By going through this death, though, they find they are able to enter into relationships which are more rewarding and life-producing. Those who enter into marriage must die to themselves, often with great fear and trepidation.

But by doing so they both enter into a new and more abundant life together.

Those suffering from a terminal disease learn to face death and yield to it. And in the moment in which they cease clinging to life they find that a new life blossoms. Likewise, the person forced to make a moral decision must die to one set of values in order to safeguard another. The preserved set of values is life-giving.

Adult children may have to die to their inability to care for their parents as they place them in nursing homes, but when they visit them there, they find that both they and their parents have found new life.

All of these passovers during our lifetime are mere preludes to the final passover which we will make when we die. At that moment, we have our last chance to trust the mystery — that it is in dying that we're born to eternal life. If we have been living the mystery all along, then death will hold little or no fear for us.

Then, too, there's always the sign of God's protective hand. During every passover God is present. It may be in a love note for the teenager, a rose for the married couple, a doctor for the cancer patient, a new insight for the person struggling with a moral decision, a smile from one's parents in a nursing home. Whatever the signs may be, they all point to God's presence and his love. Wherever blood is shed and death confronted, God is there, leading us through our passover to new life in him.

Meditation: When did you most recently experience a passover? What was the situation? What blood was shed? To what did you die? What new life did you discover? What was the sign of God's presence with you?

Prayer: God of Israel, when your people were held in slavery, you set them free through the blood of the passover lamb. Through the suffering, death, resurrection, ascension, and gift of the Spirit of Jesus, the new passover lamb, you established the paschal mystery. When we are confronted with death and life, give us the strength to trust the mystery of Jesus. Guide us with your Spirit through our daily dyings to the abundance of life which you share with Jesus and the Holy Spirit, who lives and reigns with you, Father, one God, forever and ever. Amen.

Activity: Identify the three great passovers of your life. For each indicate the situation, the blood that was shed, the death you endured, the new life you discovered, and the sign of God's presence with you through it all. What have you learned from these experiences?

The Passion of the Lord

THE PRICE

Scripture: We had all gone astray like sheep,
    each following his [or her] own way;
But the LORD laid upon him the guilt of us all.
Though he was harshly treated, he submitted
    and opened not his mouth;
Like a lamb led to the slaughter
    or a sheep before the shearers,
he was silent and opened not his mouth.

(Isaiah 53:6-7)

Mass: Isaiah 52:13 - 53:12; Hebrews 4:14-16, 5:7-9;
John 18:1-19:42

Reflection: Anyone who is willing to stand up for values today must also be willing to pay the price: suffering. Values cost. Sometimes values cost lives.

For example, the individual who prizes the value of honesty must be willing to stand up for the truth when it is very inconvenient to do so. When others have strayed, like sheep, from the path of truth, it is easy for the person who verbally acknowledges honesty as a value to forget it. In the midst of one's peers, if a person is asked, "Do you know who is responsible for this?" it is much easier to answer, "No, I have no idea," than it is to provide a name. In this situation the price to pay for honesty might be ostracism and verbal abuse.

Another value that many prize is family togetherness. However, while its importance easily rolls off the lips of most people, how many are willing to pay the price to insist on it when members of the family begin to wander away? Some families declare, "It's important to get together a few times a week for a meal." But when one of the parents has to work late or one of the children has a basketball game, orchestra practice, play rehearsal, or any one of another hundred things to do, who will sacrifice his or her activity in order to be present at the family meal?

Catholics talk about the importance of setting Sunday aside as a day of rest. But how valuable is Sunday as the Lord's Day? To uphold the value of Sunday in the face of a society that has made the weekend a time for shopping at the local mall, mowing the yard, painting the house, tilling the garden, and a host of other work projects means that a person must be willing to pay the price. If Sunday is not just another day during the week then it must be made different by attendance at church and a conscious effort to make it a holy day of rest. Otherwise, what is its value? The price to pay is the sacrifice of an hour or so of one's time to attend church, no shopping and no work. Such projects can generally be put off for another evening or a Saturday.

Values cost. There's a price involved in upholding any value. The person who is willing to pay the price often feels like a lamb led to the slaughter. Everyone else beckons the individual to sacrifice the value and join the rest of the crowd. The person who believes in values refuses to accept the invitation and stands silently for what he or she holds dear. One's example is often more eloquent than one's words. By keeping quiet, a person says a lot at times about what values he or she treasures and the price he or she is willing to pay to maintain them.

Meditation: When did you most recently discover yourself standing up for a value? What was it? What did it cost you? How do you feel about yourself for doing this?

Prayer: Lord God, when we had gone astray like sheep, each following his or her own way, you sent your Son, Jesus, to reveal to us the values of your kingdom. Though he was harshly treated, oppressed, and condemned, he remained faithful. Through his suffering, death, and resurrection, he has given us an example. Give us the strength to stand up for the values for which Jesus was willing to die. Enable us to always walk in the light of his truth. We ask this through our Lord Jesus Christ, your Son, who lives and reigns with you and the Holy Spirit, one God, forever and ever. Amen.

Activity: Make a list of three values in which you strongly believe. Identify a situation when you had to stand up for each of these. Did you remain faithful to them? What price did you have to pay? You might also want to list occasions when you sacrificed the value in order to avoid standing alone.

The Easter Vigil

BAPTISM

Scripture: Are you unaware that we who were baptized into
Christ Jesus were baptized into his death? We were
indeed buried with him through baptism into death,
so that, just as Christ was raised from the dead by
the glory of the Father, we too might live in newness
of life. For if we have grown into union with him
through a death like his, we shall also be united with
him in the resurrection.   (Romans 6:3-5)

Mass: Genesis 1:1 - 2:2; Genesis 22:1-18; Exodus 14:15 - 15:1;
Isaiah 54:5-14; Isaiah 55:1-11; Baruch 3:9-15, 32 - 4:4;
Ezekiel 36:16-28; Romans 6:3-11;
(Year A) Matthew 28:1-10;
(Year B) Mark 16:1-8;
(Year C) Luke 24:1-12

Reflection: Unless we were baptized as an adult, most of us
have no recollection of the day of our baptism. A few weeks after
birth, a child is normally brought to the parish church, where,
with parents, godparents, and others present, the priest, deacon,
or other delegated minister brings it to the baptismal font where
he or she is initiated into the body of Christ and the paschal
mystery. Thus, baptism becomes the most important event of
one's life.

In order for the meaning of baptism to be clearly understood, the signs of the event have to be illuminated and not
merely explained. In the early days of the Church many baptismal pools were built into the floors of the meeting places of
Christians. They were about the size of an open grave with one
set of steps leading down into the watery tomb and another
leading out. Those who went down into the water were said to
die and, at the same time, to be anointed with the Holy Spirit.
Once they died by going under the water, they were raised up to
new life and exited the pool.

This being buried like Christ Jesus and being raised like
him was further signified with clothing. Those not yet baptized
stripped down before entering the waters. They shed the clothes
of a former way of life. After dying and rising, they were clothed
in new white robes to indicate the new life that they were now
beginning to live.

In the course of time still another sign was added to the
ritual of baptism. After coming up out of the water, the newly
baptized were anointed with Chrism Oil, a sign of the Holy
Spirit. Not only had they been baptized with water, but they
were anointed with the Holy Spirit as well. The name of the oil,
Chrism, got its name from Christ. Just as Christ was anointed
with the Holy Spirit at his baptism in the Jordan River, so are
people christened or "Christed" with the Holy Spirit at their
baptism.

The simple act of pouring a little water over someone's
head or dabbing on a little oil or clothing them in baptismal
robes only hints at the full significance of baptism, the fullness of
which will only gradually be revealed. The sacrament initiates a
person into a lifetime of dying and rising.

Baptism begins a lifetime celebration of the paschal
mystery — suffering, dying, rising, ascending, receiving the
Holy Spirit. Every day contains some amount of suffering. Every
day there is some type of dying: to one's own ideas, one's own

way of seeing or doing things, one's own selfishness. When the dying is done, new life is experienced. With this new life comes a new vision. And it may suddenly occur to a person that all of this has occurred through the activity and presence of the Holy Spirit.

Yes, baptism initiates us into a lifetime process of growing in union with Jesus. It conforms us to his image, so that just as he suffered, died, rose, ascended, and shared the gift of the Holy Spirit with us, so too do we who are baptized into the paschal mystery. Day by day we are molded into other Christs.

Meditation: When have you most recently experienced the paschal mystery? After having experienced it, in what ways do you now resemble Jesus more?

Prayer: God of mystery, in the life and death of Jesus, your Son, you initiated the paschal mystery. Through baptism into his body, you have enabled us to share in this great gift. Give us strength to endure our suffering. Be with us when we die. Raise us up to new life and new vision. And continue to anoint us with your Holy Spirit. Enable us to trust the mystery as you conform us into the image of Jesus, who lives and reigns with you and the Holy Spirit, one God, forever and ever. Amen.

Activity: What is the date of your baptism? If you do not know, make it a point to find out. Record what you consider to be the three most powerful experiences of the paschal mystery in your life. How are each of these related to baptism?

Cycles A, B and C

NO PARTIALITY

Scripture: Peter proceeded to speak and said, "In truth, I see that God shows no partiality. You know . . . what has happened all over Judea, beginning in Galilee after the baptism that John preached, how God anointed Jesus of Nazareth with the holy Spirit and power. He went about doing good and healing all those oppressed by the devil, for God was with him. We are witnesses of all that he did both in the country of the Jews and in Jerusalem. They put him to death by hanging him on a tree. This man God raised on the third day."

(Acts 10:34, 36-40)

Mass: Acts 10:34, 37-43; Colossians 3:1-4 or 1 Corinthians 5:6-8; John 20:1-9

Reflection: As so often happens, an individual may favor one person over another. Because of this bias, a grandmother may give two pieces of candy to one grandchild and only one to another. An employer may offer a large raise to one employee and a rather small one to another. Because of one's past credit rating, a bank may refuse one person a loan but gladly give one to the next person in line. Such favoritism abounds in the world.

This is not true, however, with God. God does not favor

one person over another. He shows no partiality. God offers every person the opportunity to believe and to be saved. Faith is a free gift given to all those who are willing to accept it. Skin color, level of education, the type of work one does, the part of the city or country one happens to live in make no difference to him. Faith is offered to everyone.

God made his Son, Jesus of Nazareth, the chosen vehicle of his self-revelation and confirmed his choice through the outpouring of his Holy Spirit at the Jordan River when Jesus was baptized. The works which followed his baptism continued to confirm that God's power was operative in him, that he and the Father were, indeed, one.

What made it difficult for people to believe that Jesus was God in the flesh was his death. The book of Deuteronomy clearly states that "God's curse rests on him who hangs on a tree" (22:23). Since Jesus was crucified, that is, hanged on a tree, then, people concluded, he could not have been a manifestation of God. Rather he was a man cursed by God.

God, however, vindicated his Son by raising him from the dead on the third day, thus fulfilling the prophecies of Scripture. Jesus was transformed, transfigured, and glorified by the Spirit of God within him. The power of God was displayed in Jesus even in death.

The new life that Jesus shares now is beyond imagining: "Eye has not seen nor ear heard, nor has it entered into the heart of man what God has prepared for those who love him." The new life that the Father gave to the body of Jesus was not the product of resuscitation. It was not the restoration of his former human life. It was a whole new way of being, beyond all previous human experience.

Adults who believe that Jesus is God's anointed one, who is filled with God's Holy Spirit and power, are baptized and enter into his death and resurrection. Symbolically, they enter the death-dealing waters of the tomb, are immersed or buried as it were, and then emerge or rise up to new life. Every time another person is baptized, he or she demonstrates that God shows no partiality. God invites all people to faith in Jesus. By believing, they begin to share in the new life of Jesus. Their complete transformation will be accomplished by God when, as God promises, he will raise everyone from the dead.

Meditation: When have you most recently demonstrated any partiality? In which ways has this affected your faith in Jesus?

Prayer: God, you sent your Son, Jesus of Nazareth, to proclaim peace to all people. You anointed him with your Holy Spirit and with power. You enabled him to do your will and to give his life by being hanged on a tree. However, you reversed the curse and raised him from the dead. Through faith and baptism you have anointed us with your Holy Spirit and given us a share in the mission of Jesus. Do not let us falter, but guide us to accomplish your will. Keep alive the expectation of new life in us that we may one day partake of the glorified life of Jesus, who lives and reigns with you and the Holy Spirit, one God, forever and ever. Amen.

Activity: Make a list of three past experiences when you overcame your partiality and discovered new life. For each, identify how God was at work in you, accomplishing good. How are you a better person, more mature in faith, because of these experiences? How has Easter happened in you?

February 22

AUTHORITY

Scripture: Tend the flock of God in your midst, overseeing it not by constraint but willingly, as God would have it, not for shameful profit but eagerly. Do not lord it over those assigned to you, but be examples to the flock. And when the chief Shepherd is revealed, you will receive the unfading crown of glory.

(1 Peter 5:2-4)

Mass: 1 Peter 5:1-4; Matthew 16:13-19

Reflection: There are two ways to look at authority: as a way of exercising power over other people, or as a way of serving them. The first view of authority is that which is practiced most; the second is the view which Jesus taught.

There is no doubt that people have authority; in any ordered society someone has to be in charge and function as the leader in order to get things done and maintain peace. In the workplace the chain of command is well defined. The employee is under the authority of the manager, who is responsible to the district superintendent, who must answer to the president of the company. In school, students are under the authority of the teacher, who is responsible to the principal, who must answer to the superintendent or the school board. In the Church, the layperson is under the authority of the pastor, who is responsible to the bishop, who must answer to the pope.

In the first view of authority, those with power lord it over those who are responsible to them. Authority enables them to control and manipulate others. In the workplace, the president of a company, for example, could fire the district superintendent because of a mistake. The superintendent could make life difficult for the manager who, in turn, could pass on his frustration to the employees.

Teachers who seek to preserve and protect their authority often end up spending their time doing this rather than teaching. When power becomes an issue in the classroom, there is little time to teach. A domineering pastor is a contradiction in terms in light of the teachings of Jesus. There is a profound difference between shepherding people and forcing them to do what you want. Shepherding requires gentle prodding, not the exertion of power.

The Feast of the Chair of Peter is a day in which we honor authority of the second type. There must be a leader. And, significantly, the leader of the Church — the pope — goes by the title of the servant of the servants of God. He is the chief shepherd of the people of God. As a servant-shepherd, he is responsible for guiding the flock entrusted to his care. His role is not that of an elevated one. In fact, it is exactly the opposite. The more authority entrusted to the true follower of Jesus, the lower one gets on the status-ladder. In our Lord's view, authority makes one a servant, not a master, of others.

Meditation: When did you last use your authority as power? When did you last use your authority as a servant? How were the results different? How were the results similar?

Prayer: God our Shepherd, you entrusted the care of your flock to your Son, our Lord Jesus Christ, who taught his followers to serve each other. Help us to use our authority wisely. By being servants of one another, may we be examples of what Jesus preached. When we are tempted to turn authority into power, remind us of his suffering and death, the supreme example of love and service. When he, the Chief Shepherd, is revealed, may we receive the unfading crown of glory. We ask this through our Lord Jesus Christ, your Son, who lives and reigns with you and the Holy Spirit, one God, forever and ever. Amen.

Activity: Name someone who recently used his or her authority as a way of exerting power over you. How did you feel about this? What did you learn from this? Which is easier: to use authority as power, or to use authority as service? Explain.

March 19

INHERITANCE

Scripture: The LORD spoke to Nathan and said, "Go, tell my
servant David, 'Thus says the LORD: Should you
build me a house to dwell in? . . . I will raise up your
heir after you, sprung from your loins, and I will
make his kingdom firm. It is he who shall build a
house for my name. And I will make his royal throne
firm forever.' "   (2 Samuel 7:4-5, 12-13)

Mass: 2 Samuel 7:4-5, 12-14, 16; Romans 4:13, 16-18, 22;
Matthew 1:16, 18-21, 24 or Luke 2:41-51

Reflection: In the ancient world every king was concerned to
have a son who would inherit his kingdom. The king's son would
carry on his name, his work, and insure that his accomplishments remained in the memory of the people of the kingdom.

   This desire to live on in the next generation is still found in
the world today. It has been modified to fit new cultures, but the
basic premise is the same. People want their name, their work,
and their accomplishments to be remembered. This is usually
insured through the writing of a will.

   A person's will indicates to whom one's belongings are to
go. A will does not usually name only one person as the sole
beneficiary of an estate, but every son and daughter is given

some share of their parents' goods. Such items as houses and furnishings, cars, various monetary sums, and other personal items are willed to one's heirs.

Through Jesus, foster son of Joseph, God has made us all his heirs. In other words, God has offered each one of us a share in his estate — eternal life in heaven. God's promise is that not only our name, but our very self, will live on. Each of us has been called by name by God; each of us bears the title child of God; each of us has been given a share in his very life.

The work that God was able to accomplish through us in our lifetime will also live on. It remains for each generation to complete the mission of spreading the good news of God's love as revealed in the life and death of Jesus. And the good we have accomplished during our lifetime will never be forgotten by God who never ceases to remember.

From this perspective it is easy to see that it is not we who build up our estate in heaven, but God who builds the house. It is he who inspires us to will and to accomplish his work on earth. And it is he who rewards the good we do with his grace and who sees to it that his accomplishments in us are never forgotten.

Meditation: What have you inherited from God? How are you going to pass this on to your heirs?

Prayer: God of David, Solomon, and Joseph, you are not interested in houses built of wood or stone. You choose to live in the hearts of those who believe in you. You make of your people living temples of your Holy Spirit. Continue to mold us into your people. Enable us to spread your name, to do your work, and to proclaim your mighty accomplishments. Let these be the inheritance we offer to those who follow us. We ask this through our Lord Jesus Christ, your Son, who lives and reigns with you and the Holy Spirit, one God, forever and ever. Amen.

Activity: Have you prepared your will? If you have, who are your heirs, and what have you left each of them? Are these the things that you really value? If you have not made a will, who will you name as your heirs, and what will you leave each of them? How can you pass on to others the name, work, and spiritual accomplishments of God in your life?

March 25

SIGNS

Scripture: Listen, O house of David! . . . The Lord himself will
give you this sign: the virgin shall be with child, and
bear a son, and shall name him Immanuel.

(Isaiah 7:13-14)

Mass: Isaiah 7:10-14; Hebrews 10:4-10; Luke 1:26-38

Reflection: Signs abound in the world. At the end of the street,
there is a stop sign. Above the entrance to almost every store,
there is a sign with the name of the establishment on it. Along
the highway, billboards display signs which advertise all kinds of
goods and services. Because there are so many signs, most
people just take them for granted. Like anything else, when
there is an abundance, there is no longer the awareness of a need.

What are some of the signs of God's presence with his
people? We say, and it is indeed true, that God is our Immanuel,
our God-with-us. But because God is not visible, we must learn
to read the signs of his presence. The danger, of course, is that
the signs of God's presence become too common and are ig-
nored or forgotten. For example, the sunrise is a sign of God's
presence. To stand before the dawn and watch as the first rays
from the orange orb of the sun spread over the eastern horizon
can fill us with a sense of purpose and courage to face a new day.

This experience of the growing light of the sun can be a moving sign of God's presence in our life.

A mountain can signal God's presence. A person can stand before the rough granite cliffs of a lofty peak or hike along the game trails around a high country meadow and listen to the silence. To stand face-to-face with the majesty of a summit which glistens with snow fields, and to feel the awesome sense of the solitude at such an elevation can speak to one of God's presence.

For some, the ocean is a sign of his presence. The feel of the sand and sea beneath your feet, the sight of the wind billowing through your clothes, the steady rhythm of the surf as it composes its own musical score is a reminder of God. To be caught up in the vastness of such an experience of the ocean is to recognize his presence.

Every day and in many places — at home, at work, or at play — God manifests his presence to us in signs. The notice may come quietly. It may come through another person. It may be proclaimed loudly through a crisis of some kind. Whatever ways in which it comes, we know that God is present. It takes the eyes of faith to recognize the signs.

Meditation: In the last twenty-four hours, name three signs of God's presence that you have recognized or experienced.

Prayer: Immanuel, our God of signs, you never abandon your people, but reveal yourself in myriad and diverse ways. The greatest of your signs was Jesus, your Son, who lived among us as a man. Attune our ears to the sounds of your silence. Open our eyes to the signs of your presence. Prepare our hearts for the warmth of your love. We ask this through our Lord Jesus Christ, who lives and reigns with you and the Holy Spirit, one God, forever and ever. Amen.

Activity: It is often during the roughest moments of life that God is present in a sign. Choose three experience from your life and identify the sign of God's presence in them. In each of these experiences, what did God announce to you?